Fay Weldon

Twayne's English Authors Series

Kinley Roby, Editor
Northeastern University

TEAS 551

FAY WELDON
Jerry Bauer

Fay Weldon

Lana Faulks

University of Oklahoma

Twayne Publishers
An Imprint of Simon & Schuster Macmillan
New York

Prentice Hall International
London • Mexico City • New Delhi • Singapore • Sydney • Toronto

Twayne's English Authors Series No. 551

Fay Weldon
Lana Faulks

Twayne Publishers
An Imprint of Simon & Schuster Macmillan
1633 Broadway
New York, NY 10019

Library of Congress Cataloging-in-Publication Data

Faulks, Lana.
    Fay Weldon / Lana Faulks.
        p. cm. — (Twayne's English authors series ; TEAS 551)
    Includes bibliographical references and index.
    ISBN 0-8057-1643-2 (alk. paper)
    1. Weldon, Fay—Criticism and interpretation. 2. Women and
literature—England—History—20th Century. I. Title. II. Series
PR6073.E374Z64 1998
823'.914—dc21   98-12895
                                                                                   CIP

This paper meets the requirements of ANSI/NISO Z3948-1992 (Permanence of Paper).

10 9 8 7 6 5 4 3 2 1

Printed in the United States of America

Contents

Preface

I was introduced to Fay Weldon in the late '80s in a graduate course in modern British fiction. She was not included in the course reading, but the professor referred to her as an experimentalist in contrast to her British contemporaries. This fact was noteworthy as critics have made much of the resistance in the contemporary British novel to follow the experimental, postmodern approaches of other international writers. Richard Todd's "The Presence of Postmodernism in British Fiction" argues with this point, citing Iris Murdoch's theories to analyze the British novel since World War II. In this essay, he refers to Fay Weldon, noting that the British critic's exclusive reading of her as a feminist "highlights Britain's reviewing establishment's fondness for the exclusively thematic approach and obscures much in Weldon's handling of narrative and technique which would align her with (international) writers more often discussed in Postmodernist terms."[1] Todd's analysis is a defense of Weldon's departure from traditional realism and a celebration of her use of parody, pastiche, and self-conscious narrators that resembles styles used by many post-1950s international writers.

With the focus of my doctoral work on the modern British novel, I felt compelled to seek out Weldon's work. What I discovered was a novelist with a genius for dark comedy and a powerful ironic vision of postmodern society. Critics tend to emphasize her feminist perspective and overlook, as Todd has suggested, her talent for storytelling and droll sense of humor. Agate Krouse says that Fay Weldon has "succeeded in writing feminist comedy, demonstrating that feminism is neither humorless nor impossible to assimilate into a work of art."[2] "Feminist comedy" aptly describes Weldon's fiction, a categorization that seems oxymoronic when purveying other feminist works of the century. Her inclusion of women in the comedy may disagree with some, and her unflattering depiction of men may disturb others, but her ironic vision is clear: human behavior is all in all fairly ridiculous.

Fay Weldon is an important novelist of the twentieth century. She has broken away from traditional narrative methods especially associated with the British novel, and she has unabashedly focused her attention on the experience of women. When one interviewer asks her "if we haven't reached a stage where there should be some post-feminist writing in which the men might be liberated?" she responds, "Let the men liberate themselves, it's time they did it."[3] This retort is indicative of Weldon's allegiance to her own fictional concerns and a delightful flippancy that characterizes her engagement with interviewers.

Weldon's literary career, spanning more than four decades, is diverse and prolific. Her success as a scriptwriter for stage, TV, and radio is daunting and her nonfiction is topically wide in scope. This study, however, deals primarily with her novels. I have attempted to uncover their thematic patterns and stylistic nuances and to trace the development of her vision as a novelist. My thematic divisions of her works, no doubt, overlap, but I have tried to identify similar concerns within groups of novels while maintaining some loyalty to chronology as well.

Acknowledgments

I would like to thank Brenda Gordon, James Gosvener, Randi Crawford, and Katie O'Halloran for their generous support and assistance on this project. They have kindly championed my efforts and made friendship seem indispensable in human endeavor.

To Brandon Kershner I offer my thanks for introducing me to Fay Weldon, and to Regina Barreca, Weldon's "official biographer," my gratitude for her words of encouragement and willingness to share her knowledge and understanding of a most enigmatic author.

Chronology

Dates reflect first publication of Weldon's works.

1931   Born Franklin Birkinshaw in village of Alvechurch in Worcestershire, England.

1936   Birkinshaw family moves to New Zealand.

1945   Returns to London and lives with grandmother, mother, and sister; attends South Hampstead High School, a convent school.

1949   Enters St. Andrews University in Scotland.

1952   Receives M.A. degree in economics and psychology from St. Andrews University.

1950s   Does market research and answers problem letters for the *Daily Mirror*. Works for the foreign office writing propaganda.

1955   Gives birth to son Nicholas.

1960   Marries Ronald Weldon, an antique dealer.

1960s   Employed as an advertising copywriter for Ogilvy, Benson & Mather, London.

1963–1977   Gives birth to Daniel, Thomas, and Sam. Family lives in Primrose Hill, a North London suburb.

1966   *The Fat Woman's Tale*, television play.

1967   *The Fat Woman's Joke*, a novel.

1968   *And the Wife Ran Away*, republication in the United States of *The Fat Woman's Joke*.

1969   One-act play *Permanence*, produced in London at the Comedy Theatre as a part of a multiact play entitled *Mixed Doubles*.

1969   Sister dies of cancer, leaving three children.

1971   Appears on David Frost's show, surprising audience by referring to feminists who are critical of the Miss World

1989   *The Cloning of Joanna May,* a novel.

1990's Marries Nicholas Fox.

1990   *Darcy's Utopia,* a novel.

1991   *Moon over Minneapolis,* a short-story collection.

1992   *Growing Rich,* a novel.

1992   *Life Force,* a novel.

1992   *Tess,* a play, presented at the Quarry Theatre in Leeds, England.

1993   *Affliction,* a novel; republished as *Trouble* in the United States in same year.

1995   *Splitting,* a novel.

1995   *Wicked Women,* short-story collection.

1995   *Rebecca West,* nonfiction.

1996   *Worst Fears,* a novel.

Chapter One
Weldon's Feminist Comedy

Biography in Brief

Facts about Fay Weldon's life are scant and elusive. Apparently the mystery surrounding her background is self-chosen, as Regina Barreca explains: "It is MORE THAN DIFFICULT to document Fay Weldon's life story because she reinvents herself biographically nearly as often as any set of questions can be posed."[1] Nonetheless, the biographical information I have included here is generally agreed upon by sources.

Fay Weldon was born Franklin Birkinshaw in the village of Alvechurch in Worcestershire, England, in 1931. Her father, a physician, moved the family to New Zealand when Fay was a child. She has said that growing up there gave "her a classlessness denied to those brought up in the Old World."[2] After her parents' divorce, she returned with her mother and sister to London when she was 14. There she grew up in a household of women—her grandmother, mother, and sister—and attended a convent school, South Hampstead High School in London, living in "fairly dire poverty" (Haffenden, 310). She describes growing up in "a house full of women" devoid of men: " 'I didn't discover men until I went to university. It came as a great shock. It didn't occur to me that men could suffer, or have the same aspirations and disappointments that I had. In fact, it took me a very long time to believe that men were actually human beings. I believed the world was female, whereas men have always believed the world is male. It's unusual for women to suffer from my delusion.' "[3] Weldon's so-called delusion is expanded upon in her works, which focus on women and relegate men to function on the sidelines, their lives and feelings not wholly realized or considered with the fervor of those of the female characters.

Her mother's side of the family is literary, her mother the author of two novels published in the '30s under her maiden name, Jepson, and Weldon's grandfather, Edgar Jepson, a critic for *Vanity Fair* and the author of adventure novels published in the '20s and '30s. Her uncle

Selwyn Jepson wrote thriller novels and films, radio plays, and television plays until the 1970s.

In 1949 Weldon entered St. Andrews University in Scotland and by 1952 had earned an M.A. in economics and psychology. Weldon says that she was admitted to the university because they believed she was male. The confusion arose from her having been "christened Franklin Birkinshaw, a name her mother invented for more or less magical reasons having to do with numerology" (Barreca, 6). Weldon describes her experience in a class on moral philosophy: "This Professor Knox of ours would remark from time to time, during lectures, that women were incapable of rational thought or moral judgment—a view held by many then and some now—and the young men would nod sagely and agree. And we young women, those being the days they were, did not take offense: we thought that was the way the world was and there was no changing it: we just assumed there was something wrong with us; we could not be properly female—that must be it" (Barreca, 188).

In her early 20s, Weldon was married for a short time, giving birth to her son Nicholas. As a single mother, Weldon experienced hardships akin to those she portrays in her fiction. She has said that "[t]he first part of my life was spent in a middle class without security, without money and without property. Being a young woman with a child to support and no father for it, you lived on what you as a woman could make, which wasn't much" (Haffenden, 311). To support her child, Weldon worked as an advertising copywriter. Describing herself as "inadequate and depressed and ignorant" during that period, she underwent analysis, which, she has said, gave her the confidence to write (Haffenden, 310). In 1960 she married Ronald Weldon, an antique dealer, with whom she has three sons. In the 1950s Weldon was a market researcher, answered problem letters for the *Daily Mirror*, worked for the foreign office writing propaganda, and wrote novels that were rejected (Dunn, 61). Later she became a successful advertising copywriter, coining the advertising slogan "Go to work on an egg." It is noteworthy that she uses the world of advertising for characters and plot contrivances. Her writing career took off in the 1960s, as she became a scriptwriter for television, theater, and radio. Since that time Weldon has produced a large number of plays for the stage, television, and radio. Her literary canon further includes 21 novels, 4 short-story collections, and 3 works of nonfiction. She published her first novel, originally a television play, in 1967: *The Fat Woman's Joke*, published in the United States as . . . *And the Wife Ran*

Away. Weldon's awards and honors include the Society of Film and Television Arts award for an episode of the *Upstairs, Downstairs* series in 1971, the Booker McConnell Prize nomination in 1979, the *Los Angeles Times* award for fiction in 1990, and numerous others. Weldon's works have been translated into more than a dozen languages (Barreca, 3), and her nonfiction has appeared in a variety of print mediums.

Regarding recent news of the author, Margaret Mitchell tells us, "In the late 1990s, she was living in London with her new husband, Nicholas Fox."[4]

Weldon's Feminist Comedy

Fay Weldon is a highly entertaining, inventive novelist with a mischievous sense of humor. Weldon's satire focuses on human folly, avoiding sentimentalism, and relentlessly magnifying human error. Weldon does not suffer fools gladly, and in her fiction, fools abound. Yet the dark underside of her humor is human suffering. Although we might laugh at the comic situation or the sardonic line, painful realities lie beneath the humorous surface of her fiction. Her ironic vision creates an amusing fictional milieu, but her social criticism is a serious matter. Marriage comes off as a comic, albeit flawed institution with husband and wife tied to each other by the basest of human emotions. Emotional dependency, economic necessity, and social urbanity keep many of Weldon's couples afloat, and infidelity and cruelty are commonplace between spouses. Her fiction acts as a corrective, amplifying the social wrongs that feed human conflict. In her novels men abuse women, women take advantage of men in retaliation, women are cruel to other women to gain power, and children remain victims of their elders. Social institutions and cultural thought unjustly favor men over women and children. Weldon relishes the mundane, exaggerating human circumstances and nuances, crystallizing our most intimate interactions so that we may look more closely at the daily act of living, in particular our relations with others. Out of these particulars, she proposes a larger social vision: the powerful lack compassion and victims will do anything to be empowered.

With the experience of women at the forefront of Weldon's fiction, its male characters take the sidelines, generally engaged in selfish pursuits. She describes women's oppression as ideological and economic: women play subservient roles as underpaid and harassed secretaries; single, impoverished mothers; and betrayed wives. To ameliorate the disadvantages of their social position, Weldon proposes that women find comfort and support from one another in a bond of sisterhood.

Mothering and pregnancy often plague Weldon's women as if they were entrapped by their own biological heritage. Childbirth, menstruation, and breast-feeding are tricks played on the female body, and motherhood is rife with difficulties. Female characters may abhor the role of mother, shunning their children, whereas others sentimentally find definition in the role, ignoring their own needs. Mothers are frequently in competition with their children, especially for the attention of the father. The idealization of motherhood counterpoised against economic disadvantages and the actual domestic responsibilities that women bear alone leaves them ambivalent toward mothering and their biological role as childbearer.

Similarly, the author's satiric treatment of birth control and abortion depicts the arbitrary nature of pregnancy. Unplanned pregnancies create difficult situations for women trying to find a more advantageous place in a society that expects them to embrace motherhood. Responsible for birth control and bearing and raising children, women suffer not only the moral quandary of choosing to have or not have children but also society's subsequent judgment of their decisions. Weldon demonstrates through ludicrous scenarios the difficulties of such choices, while also showing that ethics are oftentimes based on a contingent set of biological forces. Men escape such decisions because of their social and biological positioning. Weldon accentuates the unfairness of this schema, suggesting that children would be better off if both father and mother shared decision making in regard to these issues and if women took less responsibility for reproduction and child rearing.

Weldon's female characters are, nonetheless, also flawed. Some misguided ones are enmeshed in an illusory world of innocence, prey to the devious, sometimes evil control of others. Self-sacrifice causes some to give up their identities in order to fulfill social expectations. Some are ruthlessly determined to gain power, causing harm to anyone, including other women and children who get in their way. The romantic scenario entraps and seduces some women; other women, loathing their bodies because they fail to match up to an idealized image, try to reconstruct themselves with plastic surgery. And perhaps most important, women make enemies of one another by competing for the attention of men. Such actions arise, however, from social otherness, from the exploitation they experience in a sexist culture. Weldon's men, on the other hand, generally practice selfishness and cruelty because of their predominant role in culture; they are accustomed to dominance, which they embrace as a way of life. Men are insensitive fathers and disloyal husbands, leaving domestic concerns to their wives. Even as Weldon's women gain some economic power through the decades, her men continue to assume that women's pursuits should take second place to theirs. And women, contrite and obliging more often than not, assume too that their jobs and aspirations hold less significance than that of their male counterparts.

To explain the flawed nature of her characters, Weldon investigates a variety of psychological and biological motives. The mysteries of the unconscious have Freudian and Jungian importance. She evokes Freud to posit children's Oedipal urges toward parents in order to deal with issues of incest and jealousies. Jung's collective unconscious is lampooned in *Trouble* via a psychotherapist whose therapy is based on Jung's theories. Weldon also asks to what degree the biological legacy of humans affects their behavior. Yet the innate, instinctual action has its cultural counterpart in her work. Cultural thought has co-opted the concept of the natural idealizing gender tendencies. What society considers to be natural for a woman is generally oppressive. In *Praxis* the title character advises women: "[W]hen anyone says to you, this, that or the other is natural, then fight. Nature does not know best; for the birds, for the bees, for the cows; for men, perhaps. But your interests and Nature's do not coincide" (133).[5] The nature-nurture debate reappears as a thematic concern. Weldon ascribes much of human behavior to upbringing, depicting unloved children who grow up to be selfish and uncompassionate. There are inherited qualities, she suggests, but children can be taught values and can prosper through loving relationships with their parents. That idea is further suggested in her tabula rasa children, whose personalities are formed by their environment alone. The evil Carl May in *The Cloning of Joanna May* was kept, when "he was little and hungry and stole, chained up in the dog's kennel in the yard, to teach him a lesson" (14). Carl's abuse leads to his abuse of others as the " 'the child who's beaten grows up to beat' " (26).

We might identify with Weldon's characters, but we would be hard-pressed to admire them. Their complicated lives might resemble our own, but we are not consoled by their actions or outcomes, though Weldon rewards women who free themselves of bad marriages or establish bonds of sisterhood. Though we might have sympathy for some because their mistakes lead to trouble and their circumstances render them hapless, most invite our recrimination for their lack of insight and their self-centeredness.

Weldon's power of invention is extraordinary. Skillfully, she uses parody to employ different fictional structures: allegory, fairy tales, science fiction, suspense, romance novels, ghost stories—no genre escapes her. Her novels often come in the form of pastiche with fragments of dialogue, a shifting of multiple narrators, and an interweaving of past and present events that undoes chronology. Supernatural elements—ghosts, channelers, psychics—populate Weldon's works, reflecting varieties of psychological perturbations or engineering plot development. Superstition, for example, may be an effete response to events that overwhelm the characters.

Narration is multivoiced. An ironic authorial voice appears in the majority of the novels, with different effects. At times the voice embodies an observation not apparent to the characters; at others it appears as a humorous aside that, though it may make us laugh, leaves us wondering whether the remark is serious or comic. This intrusive narrator may be a sententious moralist with a dark sense of humor, one who sees culture from a broad perspective, and whose discernment transcends the novel's ongoing events, or she may be an observer who relates events as she sees them. The authorial voice may also adopt the language and attitude of a character who is self-deceived. David Lodge refers to this technique as "a polyphonic medley of styles, or voices."[6] Further, point of view is seldom singular in Weldon's work but involves the perceptions of more than one woman. Frequently, the author unhinges the narrative from voices altogether, inserting dialogue that appears in script form. This technique may reveal personality and personal relationships in the most intimate of moments when people say hateful, secretive things to one another, or perhaps it conversely captures the inanity or cruelty of conversation at social events. This dialogical framing reveals the psychology of the characters who seem to speak subliminally, if not from the unconscious, from somewhere below the surface of propriety. Conversation between husbands and wives sounds painfully real, as if long-term intimacy had unleashed their deepest fears and longings.

Weldon has been lauded for her attention to detail. John Braine says, "She is never vague. She never leaves the reader wondering how old a character is, what they look like, what specifically they are doing. We are told what her characters eat and drink, how they earn their living, how their houses are furnished. She doesn't overload the narrative with detail; she understands what few novelists understand, that physical details are not embellishments on the story, but the bricks from which the story is made."[7] Details are a distinctive force in Weldon's fiction: her narratives evoke a sensual world in which people eat, have sex, and carry on the pedestrian activities of everyday life. Her concern with the characters' physical world is apparent in the following passage from *Female Friends,* which describes the childhood home of Grace, a central character: "The Songfords lived in Ulden, in a solid Edwardian house called The Poplars. It had a good-sized garden, a wind-break of poplar trees, a swing for the children, a tennis court, large attics, a gardener, a daily, a pantry full of bottled fruits and jams, living rooms with chintzy curtains and squashy sofas, Persian rugs, Chinese carpets, much bamboo furniture, Eastern bric-a-brac, mementos of the Indian army from which Grace's father had been cashiered, and one small bookcase containing the *Encyclopaedia Britannica* in twelve volumes, some guide books, an atlas, two novels by Dornford Yates, and three thrillers by Sapper and *The Light that Failed* by Rudyard Kipling" (21). One noticeable characteristic of Weldon's use of language is her boldness, her willingness to turn an honest phrase without the desire to please. Her descriptions of sex and the body, for example, are vivid and explicit as in the following line from *Worst Fears:* "It was as if the earthy spirit of her cunt rose up to issue from her mouth" (7). *Life Force* brings us a tale of "Leslie Beck's cock, or dong, or dick, or willy, or whatever awed, affectionate, familiar or derisory word you choose to call it by" (85). In these examples Weldon uses the raw expletives of street language for humorous effect. One reviewer refers to such language as "raunchy," and another to her use of the *f* and *c* words, as "salty, but it's the only spice in her rack, and that makes for a shriveled reading experience." Weldon's use of language is frequently parodic, an imitation of clichés and sentiments found in popular magazines and romance fiction. David Lodge points out that this kind of imitation is what Bakhtin called " 'doubly-oriented discourse': the language simultaneously describes an action, and imitates a particular style of speech or writing" (Lodge, 129). Similarly, Weldon's use of profanities and sexual "ease" mimics the contemporary language of society. Her clichés imitate the way real people talk.

Weldon's bold use of language leads her astray sometimes, but at other times to phrasing that surprises us with its clarity and wit. Her refusal to be abashed, to please the critics, is the crux of her talent. In *Worst Fears* this metaphor describes the feeling of grief: "She imagined that an animal in a bad situation, caught in a trap, in a vivisection lab, lost and hungry, would feel no worse than this. If you had a poor memory, no language skills, very little sense of time, and a limited understanding of cause and effect, this was what it would be like. Buffered by these constraints, you would not suffer too much" (13). The comparison is humorously brutal, but apt. Weldon writes about women who try to please, something she simply does not try to do. As she has said: "As a writer I'm not conscious of what Virginia Woolf described as 'the angel in the house.' I'm not conscious of someone breathing over my shoulder and whispering: 'Be good. Please men.' As a writer, I can free myself from the need to be liked, appreciated and not disapproved of by men."[8]

Weldon's brand of feminism puzzles those who find her portrayal of women unsavory. To those who find her male characters dark portraits, she (in a number of interviews) reminds them that she also creates unflattering portrayals of women. Critic Ann Hebert argues, "That no one is innocent, man or woman, complicates her searing critique of the current construction of heterosexual gender relations and makes her novels unsettling to conservatives and feminists alike."[9] Weldon's feminist perspective evades categories, though her viewpoint appears more pragmatic than ideological. Her fiction scrutinizes the actual social condition of women, their economic well-being, for example, rather than offering homilies about female liberation. In a recent interview she says that "I think society has been informed by feminism to a very large extent, but to what extent individual women are, I don't know. It would be very disappointing if young women weren't feminists, but once you go have babies and are face to face with the world and try to earn a living and do everything, you tend to become rather pragmatic in your view. It's easier if you're a woman with children to be kept by a man than try to support yourself. Anyway, young women these days would have to define feminism for me. I don't know quite what is meant by it."[10] Such statements characterize Weldon's concern with how the concepts of gender equity have impacted women's lives in the workplace and at home.

Weldon's narrative style has undergone myriad changes over the years. Never satisfied with a singular approach to style, she creates diverse narrative structures that surprise us with their ingenuity. She continues to use allegory and parody for many of her novels, with greater control in the last two decades. Two of her recent novels, though, *Trouble* and *Worst Fears,* return to the domestic sphere and the intricate details of married life. Noticeably, their realistic plots and controlled characterizations have more in common with traditional realism than earlier novels. Beginning in the late '80s, Weldon's female characters rise in social status, becoming writers, actors, and entrepreneurs. But even with their economic success, women remain in roles subservient to men, oftentimes fearing that their ascendancy in the social order will cost them their relationships. In *Leader of the Band* (1988), a female astronomer hides her success from her new lover in fear of losing his affection. In *Trouble* (1993), the female protagonist who has written a successful novel allows her husband to thwart her rising celebrity. Though the economic situations of women have changed in Weldon's later novels, their relationships have not. Social conditions may have improved for women, but in the domestic realm, little has changed.

Chapter Two

The Early Works:
Searching for Identity

We women, we beggars, we scrubbers and dusters, we do the best we can
for us and ours. We are divided amongst ourselves. We have to be, for
survival's sake. (*Female Friends*, 194)

Weldon's first three novels establish the fictional themes, styles, and
structure that she will repeat in later novels. Their dark humor describes
the experience of women in contemporary society, especially the conflict
between traditional definitions of womanhood and the search for personal identity. The social milieu predates the women's movement,
reflecting the conventional female roles of the '40s, '50s and '60s, when
the range of women's lives was limited to that of mother and wife in the
domestic realm or that of low-paying, subservient positions in the workplace. These novels are about powerless women who have little personal
identity and few economic resources. Unmarried mothers are especially
disadvantaged with the sole responsibility of raising children and stig-
matized for their sexual misconduct. *Down Among the Women* focuses on
20-year-old Scarlet, who becomes pregnant after her first sexual experience and then must raise the child without the help of the father. Married women have more financial security but are preempted by husbands and children who define them. Lack of money and opportunity
forces the female characters to figuratively prostitute themselves by
using sex and outright deception to find advantage in the only ways
available to them. Women will in fact betray one another to promote
their own self-interest. In . . . *And the Wife Ran Away,* Phyllis chases after
Esther's husband with skillful deliberation, unmoved by any ethical con-
siderations. Weldon portrays the competition of women as an offshoot of
their limited social roles and lack of personal identity. Yet she describes
these cutthroat women as wrong thinking and in league with their
oppressors. These novels also show women supporting one another to
alleviate difficulties. Creating networks of women, these stories demon-

strate how female allegiance can be a source of strength. Forgiveness is a significant theme in *Female Friends*, as the narrator explains, "I have been understanding and forgiving my friends, my female friends for as long as I can remember" (5).

. . . And the Wife Ran Away

Weldon's first novel, *The Fat Woman's Joke*, published in the United States with the title . . . *And the Wife Ran Away*, embodies the elements of feminist comedy that imbue all of her works. Written in 1967, the novel was originally a feminist play written for television. Weldon has said that when she wrote the novel she was unaware of the women's movement (Dunn, 55). That is surprising considering how profoundly the novel reflects the feminist issues of the era. The situation of female characters, trapped in the traditional female roles of the '50s and '60s, is treated ironically as they struggle to find love and happiness in an antagonistic world. The protagonist, Esther, experiences recognition of her oppressed status without the advantage of feminist ideology. Her rebellion, however, against the traditional role of mother and wife, embodies a feminist argument with an intelligent, humorous analysis of gender roles and the war between the sexes. Esther's feminism is a product of self-discovery, enlightenment that comes from personal experience rather than treatises. Her rudimentary understanding of the female predicament presages later novels in which the female characters espouse ideas that reflect the changing social views of gender. Esther's sage and boundless vitriol carries the novel's humor, arising from her epiphany and attempt to escape her status of middle-class, overweight housewife. The joke referred to in the original title is that of Esther, who has run away from her husband, moving to a squalid basement flat where she has resigned herself to eating obsessively: "She ate frozen chips and peas and hamburgers, and sliced bread with bought jam and fishpaste, and baked beans and instant puddings, and tinned porridge and tinned suet pudding, and cakes and biscuits from packets" (1). The story of why she has run away unfolds in a narrative addressed to her friend Phyllis, who has come to ask her to return home. The story she tells Phyllis is one of "patterns but not endings, meanings but no answers, and jokes where it would be nice if no jokes were" (10).

Esther and her husband, Alan, are an overweight, middle-class couple whose placid lives disintegrate one evening during a dinner party at

the home of Phyllis and her husband, Gerry. After an evening of con-
tentious repartee, Alan tells Esther she's "a little too fat" (22), announc-
ing that they are going on a diet tomorrow "to fight back middle-age"
(25). Esther explains to her friend the significance of this decision:
" 'Alan and I were accustomed to eating a great deal, of course. We all
have our cushions against reality: we all have to have our little treats to
look forward to. With Gerry it's looking forward to laying girls, and
with you it's looking forward to enduring it, and with Alan and me it's
eating food. So you can imagine how vulnerable a diet made us.' "(15)
The austere diet leads to a hunger that makes them both irascible and
argumentative. This physical hunger takes on metaphorical significance
as the couple's desire for food leaves them with a personal emptiness.
Alan's discontent and hunger move him to have an affair with his secretary, Susan, while Esther remains at home bored and lost without her
routine of eating, shopping, and preparing food for her husband. Their
irritability leads to a brutal argument followed by Esther's leaving home
after Alan calls her a "fat slut" and tries to choke her (176).

As Esther relates the story of her disintegrating marriage, she assesses
female identity as it is defined by social power structures. The collapse of
her marriage gives Esther a broader vision of the institution, as she bit-
terly explains to Phyllis: " 'Marriage is too strong an institution for me.
. . . It is altogether too heavy and powerful.' And indeed at that
moment she felt her marriage to be a single steady crushing weight, on
top of which bore down the entire human edifice of city and state, learning and religion, commerce and law, pomp, passion and reproduction"
(4). In this humorous, hyperbolic statement, Esther refers not only to
the heaviness of her marriage, but also to the burden of social power systems. The warp and woof of this flawed institution is deeply cultural:
marriage at its core is motivated and constructed by the desire for
money and power. Marriage has significance beyond the personal; it is
layered with meaning that reaches into the very source of civilization.

The weight metaphor finds further expression in the novel's fat jokes.
By gaining weight, Esther retaliates against the institution that has
been weighing on her. Fat gives the novel a carnivalesque quality. In
contemporary society the fat, especially women, are laughable and
pathetic, whereas the thin are prized and desirable. Esther uses this cultural bias to play her own joke. Rather than trying to achieve a thin,
socially valued body, she chooses to eat and grow fatter, rebelling
against the idealization of the thin female body, an image she recognizes

is an empty one. As Esther tells her story to Phyllis, a thin woman, she berates her for believing that size determines happiness: " 'I suppose you really do believe that your happiness is consequent upon your size? That an inch or two one way or the other would make you truly loved? Equating prettiness with sexuality, and sexuality with happiness? It is a very debased view of femininity that you take, Phyllis' " (5). Phyllis comes off badly in the novel because she equates happiness with thinness and physical beauty. Her entrapment in a socially constructed view of femininity has led to unhappiness and a miserable marriage with a husband who dominates her. She is "neat, sexy and rich; invincibly lively and invincibly stupid" (2). Phyllis's extreme adherence to the feminine ideal is portrayed as shallow and vain. Her thin body reflects her altogether lack of mental weight. Reversing social stereotypes in which female beauty and thinness are valued above other characteristics, including intelligence, the novel transposes this view, making the thin woman the fool.

Food and intelligence, on the other hand, are coupled and championed in Esther's rebellion. After the humiliating experience of the diet, she understands the distorted social view of the female body. Discovering that Phyllis has had breast augmentation, Esther chides her, saying that breasts are "mammary glands, milk producers, not male exciters" (129). The diet brings Esther to see the female body as a fetishized social construct. Growing fatter, she rejects the idealized image, rebelling against desirability, a central motivation of women, which they mistake for being loved. With her clearer vision Esther sees human beings as motivated by biological urges. She tells Phyllis that men are the enemy of women, criticizing her friend for wearing trousers: " 'Women should aspire to be as different as possible from them. You should wear a skirt as a matter of principle. There must be apartheid between the sexes. Men and women should unite only for the purpose of rearing children' " (103). Eating, too, because it is necessary for human existence, becomes an apt metaphor for biological necessity, as she explains to Phyllis: " 'I don't really eat, . . . I scavenge. I am trying to clear up the mess that surrounds me, like a cat cleaning up after having kittens" (101). In these lines, Esther rejects the symbolic world of sex and gender relations, favoring base, physical human motives. Radically, she redefines these motives returning to instinct as a basis for human behavior. Patricia Waugh describes this act as one of "regression . . . to the orality of infancy: gobbling, gorging, taking in."[1] As Esther returns to infancy, she rejects the role of feeder, choosing to feed herself as a child in need of emotional nourishment.

Food has given stability to Esther and Alan's marriage, as she explains to Phyllis: "All day in his grand office Alan would sip coffee and nibble biscuits and plan his canteen dockets and organize cold chicken and salad and wine for working lunches, and all day at home I would plan food, and buy food, and cook food, and serve food, and nibble and taste and stir and experiment and make sweeties and goodies and tasties for Alan to try out when he came home" (15). As the diet disturbs the complacency of their marriage, it begins to collapse. Alan's hunger indeed leads him to an affair with Susan, who, like a predator, recognizes his vulnerability. In a second narrative, Susan tells her friend Brenda about the affair. Susan exemplifies the aggressive, competitive young woman who considers husband-stealing a sport. Brenda has moral scruples about having an affair with a married man, saying that she would "worry about his wife." In response Susan explains her callous view on the subject: "You are different from me. You are fundamentally on the side of wives, and families. I don't like wives, on principle. I like to feel that any husband would prefer me to his wife. Wives are a dull, dreadful, boring possessive lot by virtue of their state. I am all for sexual free enterprise. Let the best woman win" (12–13). Susan's cold-minded philosophy pits woman against woman in competition for the attention and possession of men. This view is a self-diminishing goal that damages female relations. At odds with one another, women form an identity through men, losing sight of their own self-worth and potential sisterhood.

Susan's desire for power masks her need for acceptance and love. The joke on Susan, like the joke on Phyllis, is that her thinness and youth will not buy her love. Alan is using her, as he admits : " '[M]y intentions toward you are entirely dishonorable. . . . This diet weakens me. You are taking monstrous advantage of a poor weak hungry man. I never thought to be an adulterer' " (78). In their final sexual liaison he actually abuses her, "penetrating every likely orifice that offered itself to his view. He slapped and bit her, pulled her breasts and tore her hair. It afforded no pleasure at all, and she suffered a mounting sense of shock and outrage" (148). Susan's sexual prowess gives her tenuous power over men. She courts desirability at the price of objectifying her own body. Alan has transferred his hunger for food to hunger for her body, treating her, as she tells Brenda, "like a whore" (150).

As Esther's story closes she describes the fight with Alan, returning to her philosophy of biological necessity: " 'I am finished. I am over. It is very simple, really. I am a woman and so I am an animal. All women are animals. They have no control over themselves. They must have children—there is no merit in it, there is no cause for self-congratulation, it is blind instinct' " (177). Here Esther interprets the end of her marriage as a response to the end of her childbearing years. Society has no need of women who can no longer procreate, as she tells Phyllis: "You're just a female animal body, fit to bear children and then be thrown away" (178). Ironically, Esther leaves the flat in order to return to mothering others. Her son Peter visits, asking her to come home, followed by Susan, who brings a lily for her to nurture. Finally, Alan too arrives, claiming that Peter needs her and blaming his relationship with Susan on the diet. Esther decides to go back home because " '[i]t doesn't seem to make much difference where one is' " (108). The novel's ending agrees with Esther's estimation of women as animals. Though Esther no longer exists to procreate, she will return to mother others, yet no longer having to conform to a social image of the body. She and Alan will return to their old routine, content and growing fat. As predicted in the lines "no endings, no answers," the novel ends unresolved, providing no clear answer to the social problems that brought Esther to her basement flat in the first place.

Down Among the Women

"Let us now raise a monument in the heart of the London Stock Exchange. Let us call it the Tomb of the Unknown Whore" (185).

The title of this novel, repeated throughout the story as a refrain, refers to the lower social and economic place of the female characters who have little opportunity to rise above their situation. The novel begins: "Down among the women. What a place to be! Yet here we all are by accident of birth, sprouted breasts and bellies, as cyclical of nature as our timekeeper the moon—and down here among the women we have no option but to stay" (1). These lines reflect the impact of biology on women's lower social status. As childbearers, their destiny is set: they have low-paying jobs and lack opportunity to gain more lucrative employment, in contrast to the towers of capitalism where power and money are to be found and where, primarily, men reap the advantages. The phrase also refers to sexual prohibitions: women are fallen when they express sexual urges and when they have sex outside of marriage. The 20-year-old central character, Scarlet, has the lowest position at the beginning of the novel, losing her virginity and becoming pregnant during a drunken interlude at a party. Unwed and pregnant, she is reviled by most of the characters, both female and male, who call her a slut and a whore. The 1950s setting explains to a degree her fallen condition. The narrator, whose identity is unknown at the beginning of the novel, comments on Scarlet's situation: "Scarlet has for some time been considered by her friends as a girl of loose sexual morality. It is not true" (40). In such commentary, the narrator undermines the characters' skewed values while offering a point of view that relinquishes Scarlet from social condemnation, emphasizing the general unfairness of pregnancy to women in contemporary society. Scarlet must not only deal with the unfortunate pregnancy without the help of the father but must suffer the misjudgment and biases of others who consider her a "loose" woman. A sexual double standard is made clear in many instances throughout the novel when the male characters' desires are considered normal and the expression of female desire is judged as immoral.

Scarlet's downcast condition as an unmarried pregnant woman is aggravated because she has no money, no training, no way to make a decent living. Wholly responsible for children, women are at a disadvantage without a man to help them economically and to give them an acceptable place in society. They are further pushed down by having to prostitute themselves to men, to become a sexual and/or domestic servant. Caught in a double bind, women must do what they can to survive while suffering the criticism of a culture in which they are both idealized and debased. "Down among the women" also includes those who have been deserted by men who have left them for younger women. As women age, society's regard for them declines further as they lose value physically as childbearers and as objects of beauty. Similarly, men often take mistresses who are younger or more compliant. Youth is the most fortuitous time for a woman: "There is nothing more glorious than to be a young girl, and there is nothing worse than to have been one. Down here among the women: it's what we all come to" (2). Women's place is biologically determined: as they age they lose status in society, economically and symbolically. To ascend from this lower, oppressed place, women often compromise their ethics. To go up, the female characters must attach themselves to a man who can economically raise them to a higher place. This impetus is magnified when a woman has children.

Female characters, in fact, have little integrity as they try to create a better life for themselves and their children through subversive measures. Female manipulation arises from this particular struggle, and though the novel does not condone such manipulation, it suggests that survival preempts personal integrity, which must sometimes be sacrificed in a world where women have limited access to economic and political power.

The social and economic disadvantages that women face make motherhood a source of ambivalence. The apparent self-sacrifice of mothering is compounded by the burden of supporting the child. The novel begins with Scarlet's problematic pregnancy. Her youth makes her naive and unprepared for the event. Her mother, Wanda, who has raised Scarlet for the most part without a father, offers her bitter commentary on the pregnancy. Wanda, who is not a model parent nor an especially bad one, is a brassy middle-aged woman who has lost all romantic sentiment for childbearing and motherhood. Like Esther, Wanda speaks out in the novel against the low position of women, though with more vitriol. At middle age she has lost all illusions of romance and marital bliss; her statements about motherhood cut through the mythical, dreamy notion of motherhood fostered in girls and young women. A primary school teacher, she has recently taught her students the Brahms lullaby, commenting: " 'Some man wrote that, and you needn't think he ever changed a nappy' " (16). Living in the postwar '50s, Wanda is surrounded by women who have adopted the conventional gender roles of their society. They please men, wasting away in self-neglect as they struggle for social acceptance. Wanda stands out as an early feminist, whose lack of concern with female roles is evident in her bawdy language as she tells Scarlet, " 'There is more to a woman . . . than her tits, her arse and her cunt, although your father was never really convinced' " (20).

Wanda and Scarlet live in a flat where Scarlet's baby will have to sleep in "the bottom drawer of the kitchen dresser, padded with crumpled newspaper and covered with white rexine" (45). In contrast, Scarlet's father, Kim, a successful adman, lives "on the fourth floor of a red-brick Edwardian block of flats off Baker Street" (27). He has taken a young wife, Susan, who is also pregnant. Not having seen her father since she was a toddler, Scarlet decides to look him up when two weeks late in her pregnancy. Finding Susan in her father's flat, Scarlet goes into labor, giving birth to Byzantia in the couple's bed. Both women are jealous of one another; Susan is jealous of Scarlet because she represents Kim's past life, while Scarlet resents Susan's economic advantages. Susan has planned a home birth with an attending doctor; Scarlet was supposed to give birth in the hospital. In an ironic twist Scarlet changes places with Susan and has her baby at Kim's home. Usurped by Scarlet, Susan has a painful, lonely birthing experience in the hospital, ignored by her husband: "Susan has a slow and difficult labour. It lasts forty-two hours. She is taken to hospital because it seems simpler to the others than to turn Scarlet out so instantly" (51).

Using the relationship between Susan and Scarlet, the novel introduces an incest theme. When Scarlet gives birth in her father's bed, she takes Susan's place, symbolically becoming her father's wife. Eventually Susan ousts Scarlet, but the competition between the two continues throughout the novel and further emphasizes the desire of women to please the father by gaining his attention or marrying him. Scarlet has, after all, become pregnant on the night her father married Susan and has "all unknowing, wanted her father's child" (89).

Scarlet's and Susan's concomitant parenthood stands in contrast to each other's. Scarlet's baby, Byzantia, is healthy and ebullient whereas Susan's Simeon is a weak, unobtrusive child. Byzantia's illegitimacy, although socially condemned, results in a healthier life for the baby. Though inexperienced and anxious, Scarlet is an affectionate mother whose position of being down in the world has kept her in touch with the reality of the body and human experience. Susan, desperate to keep herself afloat and proper in married life, is unhappy and out of touch with her body, raising her son in an artificial, strained way. Her concern with propriety leads to unhappiness and awkward mothering. Marriage, the most desirable institution for women in 1950s society, proves to be a prison for Susan.

Scarlet's friends provide subplots to the central plot of Scarlet's pregnancy and motherhood. The phrase "Down among the girls" refers to those who have yet to be mothers, implying a naïveté about the true nature of motherhood. These friends—Jocelyn, Helen, Sylvia, and Audrey—have compassion for Scarlet but also judge her for her supposed loose morals. They feel superior to her, adhering to the social view that a pregnant, unmarried woman is indeed fallen. Yet all of the girls experience bad love affairs and marriages—they receive their comeuppance in painful ways—contributing to their growing awareness of the unfair social position of women. That the girls have yet to become pregnant is a matter of luck: "Contraceptives. It is the days before the pill. Babies are a part of sex. Rumours abound. Diaphragms give you cancer. The Catholics have agents in the condom factories—they prick one in every fifty rubbers with a pin with the Pope's head on it. You don't get pregnant if you do it standing up. Or you can take your temperature every morning, and when it rises that's ovulation and danger day" (13). The girls continue to have sex yet remain anxious about pregnancy. Jocelyn "takes no precautions at all. . . . Every month she doubts her own disbelief, is clenched and pale with anxiety, until her female flow once more underlines her female condition, and the cycle starts another round" (14–15). This cyclical process of the female body, a natural biological condition, becomes a source of agony, fear, and superstition of the women, who are wholly responsible for birth control and for the random, unwanted pregnancy. Biological destiny, then, results in women's lower social status. They want to please men by having sex with them but must also agonize over the unwanted pregnancy that may lead to having a child out of marriage or to an illegal abortion. Sylvia, for example, having had an abortion at 15, tells her psychiatrist that "[e]verything went wrong because of that" (198). In Weldon's view there is no fortunate circumstance that is anything but temporary for women in society. If they choose conventional roles of propriety and self-sacrifice, they end up miserable. If they act in antisocial ways, they are turned out by society or feel guilt for having made mistakes they must live with for the rest of their lives.

Although conflicts exist between Scarlet and her friends, they genuinely care for one another, even though it is difficult to maintain female friendships in a society that promotes competition among women. The conflict between loving one's friends and fulfilling social expectations creates tension between the women, but that the novel is written from the point of view of one of the friends suggests that women can find sympathy for one another, rejecting rivalry and social expectations. The identity of the first-person narrator is not revealed until the end of the novel when we learn it is a friend, Jocelyn, whose retrospective transcends any bitterness that earlier existed among the group. Weldon's choice of one of the friends to tell the story insists on the ability of women to understand one another, to be able to tell another's story with aplomb and goodwill. Jocelyn is a trustworthy narrator, as we believe throughout the novel, who tells an honest story of her friends with their flaws and misfortunes, as well as her own. We discover that her story is one of remorse, having scalded her son, Edward, in the tub, as she tells Scarlet: " 'I was bathing him, and forgot to put the cold water in, and lowered him into scalding water. There is, of course, no such thing as an accident. I did it on purpose to my child, because he looked like Philip' " (213). Jocelyn's guilt about her child has caused her great pain, but her suffering leads to understanding and knowledge as she realizes: "One can learn, at least. One can go on learning until the day one is cut off" (215).

It is telling, however, that Scarlet, who begins the novel as the lowest of the group, slowly rises above her situation, gaining personal strength. Marrying Edwin, an older man, she tries to conform to the role of a subservient housewife, hoping to better Byzantia's life. Bored in Lee Green, she eventually leaves, allowing Edwin to support her for a while. But this obligation proves to be too cumbersome and she leaves again, calling Edwin " 'a stupid, impotent, elderly old dribbler' " (166) and deciding to attend college. She later finds Alec, a man her own age, whom she marries: "Alec has inherited a good deal of money. Scarlet has her sociology degree. She is hoping for a lectureship at the London School of Economics" (199). Byzantia, however, becomes the strongest female voice in the novel's final pages. A conversation between Byzantia and Scarlet offers hope that a new generation of women will rise above the status of the previous one. Throwing a party for her mother's friends, Byzantia, now 18, tells her mother that she will not offer the friends marijuana, because she considers them "too unstable." Scarlet responds, "We haven't done too badly. . . . 'There's me with Alec, Jocelyn here with her Ben, Sylvia with her Peter, and I daresay Audrey will bring her Editor, if she thinks he'll have a bad enough time. And even your step-grandmother Susan will be able to bring your uncle Simeon.' " Byzantia replies: "You amaze me. . . . Fancy seeing success in terms of men. How trivial, with the world in the state it's in" (216). Byzantia, a child of the '60s, is blessed by a society in revolt against social conventions. The difference between the generations of women is illustrated in these lines: "Byzantia like her grandmother Wanda, is a destroyer, not a builder. But where Wanda struggled against the tide and gave up, exhausted, Byzantia has it behind her, full and strong" (216). Here the novel offers hope that social reformation may change the conventional roles of women. Byzantia has reaped the benefits of Wanda's liberated views; Wanda, at a less progressive time, began the thinking process that Byzantia has inherited. What Wanda will never have, Byzantia may. She has the advantage of the changing times and a grandmother who fought at a time when such rebellion invited disdain. As the novel began so it ends—"Down among the women. We are the last of the women" (216). The last women are those of the older generation who will be replaced by the younger ones such as Byzantia with their liberated views of female identity. Agate Krouse describes the novel's positive message: "Such blending of the terrible and the ridiculous is one of the major reasons why a novel filled with the pain endured by women—lack of love, abandonment, violence, and death account for three-fourths of the events—is neither painfully depressing nor cheerfully sentimental. It also places Weldon in the mainstream of contemporary fiction" (Krouse, 15).

Female Friends

Female Friends echoes *Down Among the Women* in its portrayal of the interconnected lives of women, their alliances, and their problematic relationships. This novel is more tightly plotted and the characters more engaging, with focus on three women—Chloe, Marjorie, and Grace. Chloe, like Jocelyn, speaks for her friends, interpreting the events of their lives. An alternating third-person point of view also carries the plot, but focuses on Chloe and her perception of events. Agate Krouse describes the strengths of the novel: "vivid imagery, a strong sense of time and place, memorable dialogue, complex events, and multiple characters that are neither confusing nor superficially observed—a rich rendering of life with brevity and wit" (Krouse, 15).

Female Friends describes the difficulties and satisfactions of female relationships. Marjorie, Chloe, and Grace have shared intimacies as children, and the bond between them continues in their adult lives. The girls' lives merge in 1940 in Ulden. Chloe and Marjorie are evacuees from the bombing of London, and Grace lives in the village, born in privilege to an aristocratic father. Grace's family takes in Marjorie, and Chloe's mother has obtained a job as a barmaid. The girls grow up together amidst difficult family lives: Chloe lives in a room in the bar with her poor widowed mother, who works for thankless employers who take advantage of her martyr-like sacrifice. Grace lives in discord with a father who abuses her self-effacing mother. Marjorie is ultimately abandoned by a self-centered mother who treats the war as a social event, entertaining and running about the country with soldiers.

The women's difficulties are explained through the accounts of their youth and the parents who raised them. Chloe posits that their unsatisfied lives originate in their upbringing: "What was it we needed? Not much. Perhaps only the fathers and mothers with which we started. Perhaps to own and not to disown us. Mothers to love us, and put themselves out on our behalf. To relinquish life as we grabbed hold of it. And smile as they did so" (45). The failure of their parents to love them has led to their present discontent, yet these women find in one another the affection that they have not found in parents or lovers. The girls' intertwining stories reflect the failure of love, or as Chloe says, "Marjorie and Grace and me. How foolishly we loved" (17). David Lodge notes that the book "portrays women as on the whole helpless victims of their wombs and hearts, craving husbands and lovers even while being abused and betrayed by them" (Lodge, 126). And as we see in the end of the novel, they care for one another as well as anyone else has in their lives. Chloe describes their torn loyalties: "We women, we beggars, we scrubbers and dusters, we do the best we can for us and ours. We are divided amongst ourselves. We have to be, for survival's sake" (194).

In the novel's present tense, the '60s, we see the middle-aged women who have evolved from these difficult pasts accounted in flashbacks over the previous two decades. Chloe's servility to her husband, Oliver, is most evident in her acquiescence to his sexual relationship with Françoise, their maid. Bullied by him, "she is in danger of becoming like her mother . . . who at least died in disgrace. Like a million, million women, shuffling and shameful to the end" (80). Marjorie is single and works as a producer for the BBC. Grace lives with Sebastian, a man 20 years younger than she, and has given up her child for Chloe to raise. The women have unsatisfying relationships with men and continue to rely on one another for support. Both Marjorie and Grace chide Chloe for continuing to tolerate Oliver, especially in his relationship with Françoise. It is Chloe, after all, who has followed in the footsteps of their compliant mothers, taking in Grace's child and two others who belong to another friend. Marjorie has forsworn a life with husband and children, and Grace remains a rebel defying convention. As Grace tells Chloe, "You're a very dangerous person, Chloe. People who stand about waiting for other people to fall to bits so they can pick up the pieces ought to be locked up. They encourage disintegration. It's time you learned to enjoy yourself, Chloe; you're too dangerous as a martyr" (232).

The women are paralyzed by their pasts, as Chloe says: "Marjorie, Grace and me. How do we recover from the spasms of terror and resentment which assail us, in our marriages and in our lives? When we lie awake in bed and know that the worst is at hand, if we do not act (and we cannot act)—the death of our children, or their removal by the State, or physical crippling, or the loss of our homes, or the ultimate loneliness of our abandonment" (113). Here, Chloe summarizes the fears that keep women tethered to their unhappy lives. They often remain in miserable relationships to ensure that they have homes for themselves and their children. Further, Marjorie, Grace, and Chloe have inherited these fears from their mothers. Chloe explains that her mother, Gwyneth, stayed at her job because "she is terrified of change. She has the feeling that though here may be bad, the other side of the hill may be a good deal worse, and that in any case patience and suffering will surely be rewarded by God" (37). Women are not only fearful of destitution, these lines suggest, but they also believe that goodness lies in self-sacrifice. Grace's mother, Esther, lives a life of servitude to her husband and child because "she has become used to it" (30).

In contrast Marjorie's mother, Helen, has chosen the path of self-interest. Doubtless, she is a bad mother, but she has rejected conventional roles to live a selfish life. Of the three mothers, she is the most admirable, as Chloe says, "Better to end like Helen unforgiving and unforgiven. Better to live like Grace, at least alive" (233). Selfishness in women is not to be derided in Weldon's fiction; in fact, it is preferable to self-sacrifice. Women who act out of self-interest usually turn out better off in her fictional schemas. Grace, for example, though not a wholly admirable character, is lauded for her attempt to resist social prescriptions. As she explains to Chloe, "Mind you, I'm the only girl who got sent to her room for hoping that Hitler would win the war. Anything for a change. I have at least kept my energy, by caring about nothing, or not for longer than a couple of hours. Morality is very devitalizing, Chloe. Look what you've done to Oliver, by being so much better than him. He hasn't done a decent day's work since you married him" (233). According to Grace, rebellion against social prescriptions is resistance to the stasis chosen by the mothers Gwyneth and Esther.

Taking action, then, is an important theme in the novel. Rebellion is preferable to complacency and acquiescence, a lesson Chloe must learn in order to escape her bad marriage. In the end Chloe does act and with the help of her friends finds a way out of her marriage. Offering Chloe occupancy of her childhood home, Marjorie facilitates her friend's escape from her oppressive marriage. Chloe leaves Oliver to start a new life, as she explains: "And as for me, Chloe, I no longer wait to die. I put my house, Marjorie's house, in order, and not before time. The children help. Oliver says, 'But you can't leave me with Françoise,' and I reply, 'I can, I can, and I do' " (237). With a reference to wedding vows, Chloe declares her victory in making a change in her life. She has avoided repeating the past behavior of her mother, who chose a life of inaction, a salient warning of the book: "What progress can there be, from generation to generation, if daughters do as mothers do?" (233).

Chapter Three

Experimenting with Form: Ghosts and Fairy Tales

I know that self-knowledge is painful. I know that to think you are a princess and find you are a beggar girl is very disagreeable. I know that to look at a prince and find he is a toad is quite shocking. (*Words of Advice*, 20)

Remember Me and *Words of Advice* rewrite stories of domestic life and romance as parables of ghosts and fairy-tale figures. The first novel, a ghost story, brings a wronged woman back from the dead to rescue her child from an evil stepmother, and in the second, the innocent are preyed upon by a fox and a witch. Evil does not prevail, however, and the young narrowly escape unfortunate circumstances. Both parables teach us that goodness and right action must come through self-awareness and through respect for the autonomy of others, especially the innocent.

Remember Me

In *Remember Me* the central character, Madeleine, dies in the course of the novel. The title asks for the other characters to remember the dead Madeleine, who haunts the rest, reminding them of her suffering and their responsibility to others. The novel develops as a broken narrative with commentary on most of the main characters, though Madeleine's story is the central one. First-person narratives inserted into the ongoing plot introduce the characters' inner voices revealing motives and psychological quandaries. Madeleine's bitterness and desire for revenge come through in her personal account; she is, after all, the wronged woman, having lost her husband, Jarvis, to a younger woman, Lily. As Madeleine's name suggests, she is mad in both meanings of the word, as this first-person narration reveals: "If I wait, if I lie quite still, warding off, fending, pretending that these attacks—of what? hate? madness?—

come from outside me, have been sent by the devil or his equivalent, and do not arise (as I know they must) from within me, being as they are the sum of every fear and sorrow, rage and despair I have ever felt, ever known; if I forbid myself to move, to act, to pick up the telephone, then the rage passes" (17). The source of Madeleine's anger is in her past suffering, in which hate and madness are commingled, indistinguishable in her emotional life. Agate Krouse notes that "[s]upernatural elements are used to underline the power of women's resentment against injustice" (Krouse, 16). Madeleine's rabid anger makes her act irrationally, even in death, as she enacts revenge on those who have wronged her. The novel resonates with irony but of a darker, less humorous kind than that of . . . *And the Wife Ran Away*. The characters' ill treatment of one another is presented with ironic statements, inviting wry laughter and amusement at the appearance of Madeleine's ghost, who returns to upset the comfortable, banal lives of the other characters.

The novel's intrusive narrator emphasizes the characters' weaknesses and their absorption in self-limiting social roles that do harm to others. Lily's role as mother and wife is described as follows: "Up gets Lily bright and early, to prepare breakfast for Jarvis her husband and Jonathan her son. Good Lily!" (7). These lines describe Lily's domestic life before it is disturbed by Madeleine's ghost. Lily's false goodness lies in her obedience and conformity to the role of mother and wife, and for some time she lives an idyllic life with her husband and child. In contrast, Madeleine, who has lost all to Lily, is described: "Up gets Madeleine, Jarvis' first wife, Lily's enemy, Hilary's mother, not so bright and not so early" (11). Madeleine, usurped by a younger woman, has lost her identity, living a despairing life outside the world of blessed routine where Lily resides. Such statements emphasize the repetitious lives of the female characters whose identities arise from the self-diminishing roles of mother and wife.

Madeleine tolerates her husband's affair until he brings a pregnant Lily into their house. Leaving one day in a vengeance, she breaks windows and takes possessions from the house. Residing in a basement apartment with her daughter, Hilary, she lives on rage and despair, calling Lily at night to make abusive comments. Returning from a Dial-a-Date rendezvous one night, Madeleine dies in a car wreck. The remainder of the plot deals with Madeleine's ghost, who is loath to leave, returning to invade the body of her husband's secretary, Margot, a weak woman. The wife of Lily and Jarvis's doctor, Margot went to bed with

Jarvis at a party and since then holds a fascination for him. She is a perfect vehicle for Madeleine's revenge because of her compliant and superficial attitude toward her own husband and life: "Margot is a good wife; she allows her husband to sap her energy and youth, and take her good nature, and feels no resentment—or thinks she does not" (21). Margot also acquiesces when Lily wants her to baby-sit her two-year-old, Jonathan. Margot complies because of her submissive nature and her desire to be close to Jarvis, but she is also more nurturing than Lily, caring for Jonathan in a way his mother cannot.

Weldon uses Madeleine's supernatural escape from death to upset the ongoing mundanity of the characters' lives. When she comes back to haunt Jarvis's house and new family, the couple experience marital conflict, revealing the superficial nature of their relationship. Jarvis questions the complexity of his marriage, and Lily recognizes that her former hatred for Madeleine when she was alive may not have been salved by the ex-wife's recent death. Lily must now become mother to Hilary, Madeleine and Jarvis's adolescent daughter, and deal with the truth that Jarvis was once in love with his former wife. Having convinced herself that Madeleine was a bad wife and that her marriage to Jarvis was loveless, Lily bristles at Jarvis's grief over Madeleine's death. Her lack of compassion and understanding leads to a brutal argument between Lily and Jarvis. Madeleine's ghost also attacks Jonathan, resulting in a blister on his heel that looks to Lily like a cigarette burn, a wound that only Lily sees as death threatening: "But how could he possibly have a cigarette burn? Lily doesn't smoke and Jarvis stopped when they were first married. When he was with Madeleine he smoked like a chimney, then and afterwards" (191). With this wound, like a hex, Madeleine tortures her nemesis, Lily, while forcing her to consider the welfare of Jonathan above her own selfish needs. In defense of her child, Lily begins to feel and act on motherly instincts that she has not previously expressed.

Possessed by Madeleine's ghost, Margot expresses animosity toward her family, which suggests that suppressed feelings have been hiding beneath her passive exterior. Madeleine's revenge and bitterness disturb the urbane surface of the couples' relationships. Madeleine's ghost in Margot's body also allows Weldon to merge two extremes of female stereotypes in one figure. The evil, sadistic woman merged with the long-suffering, compliant one combines two extremes of female identity, a dichotomy that plays on the social view of women as either good or bad, a split identity with which women must wrestle in their attempt to fulfill social expectations. This divided sense of self creates an internal war within the female characters as they try to forswear the dark side and conform to the good. The apparent good girl, though, has a bad side, which when it erupts causes pain to others; her suppressed aggression is hostile and lacking in compassion, the polar opposite of what women are supposed to be. A society that asks women to be "good" mothers, daughters, and wives forces women to hide imperfections and discontent. That suppression eventually erupts in hostility as women, through self-sacrifice and denial, try to fill roles impossible to achieve. Margot exemplifies a female character whose self-sacrifice and adherence to the conventional role of mother and wife hide deeper longings and personal needs. When she rebels, with the help of Madeleine's ghost, she turns mean, calling Lily in the middle of the night as Madeleine once did: " 'You bitch,' says Madeleine/Margot in her new hoarse voice, in response to Lily's best fluty hostess tones. 'You filthy murdering bitch. You stole Jarvis. You shan't have Hilary too' "(175).

Weldon's concern with the middle-class milieu of twentieth-century England is evident in her portrayal of social events—parties, dinners—which are always unpleasant, with characters expressing their discontent in hateful dialogue, or with discontent shown through narrative that indicates the characters' true motives. In *Remember Me* Weldon introduces Judy and Jaime, a couple who, once in love, have now turned resentful and bitter. During a dinner party at Jarvis and Lily's, they make everyone uncomfortable, turning the party into an absurd event. Judy and Jaime appear as a foil to Jarvis and Lily's relationship, which has yet to be tested by the difficulties of a long-term relationship. Comically, it is at this dinner party—the turning point of the novel, the point at which the lives of the central characters begin to collapse—that Madeleine's ghost appears. As a cold wind blows through the house, Margot becomes hysterical and "slaps at her right leg with a curious waving, banging movement, as if the leg has no business being there; the other hand hits and hits her chest" (95). Margot's actions are in response to the effects of the crash on Madeleine's body. In contrast to her previously demure behavior, Margot creates a social disturbance, her embarrassment expressed in an interior voice: "I am Margot the doctor's wife, fresh from public humiliation. What will they think of me? How will I face them again?" (97). This initial concern with appearances fades as Madeleine's presence becomes a stronger force in Margot's personality.

A thematic concern of the novel is the suffering the children experience because of their parents' wrongdoing. Hilary, an unattractive adolescent girl, is loved though neglected by her mother, who is preoccupied with her desire for revenge. Lily resents Hilary because she represents Jarvis's former life, and in retaliation Lily mistreats her stepdaughter, taking her to a salon to have her long blond hair cut. This modification highlights Hilary's bad features and is a symbolic act of disempowerment. When Madeleine dies, Lily sends Hilary to school, saying " 'You have to carry on. We all have to carry on' " (125). Such insensitivity demonstrates Lily's selfish concerns; she is indifferent and indeed unfeeling toward the children. Madeleine, however, makes up for her failure to properly care for Hilary when she returns as a ghost to ensure that her daughter lives with Margot and Philip. In fact, the primary purpose of Madeleine's ghostly return is to make sure that Hilary receives care and finds a place where she is wanted. When Philip suggests that Hilary come live with them, Madeleine leaves Margot's body and is put to rest.

Jonathan, too, suffers at the hands of the adults. Lily pays little attention to him, and he becomes a target of Madeleine's vengeful ghost, who uses him to get back at Lily and Jarvis for the harm they have done to Madeleine. Because of his parents' neglect after finding that Madeleine has died, Jonathan picks up a whiskey bottle and gets drunk. At another point he almost falls off the stairs. No real harm comes to Jonathan, but the close calls suggest that his parents are playing a dangerous game with destiny. Neglect of children could result not only in emotional harm but in physical death. Jonathan is fortunate, though, to have Hilary and Margot to love and comfort him, and to provide the nurturing that his parents do not.

The novel's supernatural machination proposes a correction for the self-centered characters. A funeral attended by the major characters brings a satisfying end to the plot, with a ritual that gives respect to Madeleine's life, and a ceremonial closure for the other characters, who must learn from her death. Jarvis and Lily both ask for her forgiveness and the characters decide to "make room" for others, suggesting that the small space of self-regard must give way for others, especially children. Lily resolves to be a better mother to Jonathan and to be kinder to Hilary, letting her choose the wallpaper for the room that will be hers on the weekends. The novel's message is clear: using children for personal power and rivalry is an abuse of love and must be replaced by self-sacrifice, the relinquishment of solipsism in order to find sympathy for others. Hilary is indeed the victor at the novel's end, as she explains: "My mother's death has set me free. My life, her death—that's the sum of what she gave me. Dying was the best thing she could do for me: this was her best and final gift" (245).

Words of Advice

Originally, *Words of Advice* was written as a play, performed in 1974. Shortlisted for the Booker Prize, the novel is structured as a double narrative, telling the story of two women, Elsa, a 19-year-old who lives with Victor, an older, married man who is separated from his wife, and Gemma, a wealthy woman in her 30s. The opening narrative centers on the visit of Elsa and Victor to the estate of Gemma and her husband, Hamish. Gemma's narrative, addressed to Elsa, is interposed within the main narrative and embodies words of advice, hence the novel's title. The meaning of the advice is not immediately clear in that Gemma's story must run its course before the reader understands her purpose in telling Elsa the story. The double narrative establishes Weldon's concern with the relationships between women, their animosity toward one another—arising out of jealousy and competition—as well as the potential help that they can give each other. There is a tension in these two impulses as the narrative develops: it is not clear whether Gemma wants to help Elsa or hurt her.

In *Words of Advice* Weldon makes a clear distinction between the wealthy and the middle class. Victor, an antique dealer, comes to the millionaires' estate at the behest of Gemma, who is seeking his advice on the "profitable disposal of certain articles of family furniture" (4). Clearly, from the beginning Gemma is in control of the situation, having invited the couple to stay the weekend and greeting them at the door in her wheelchair. Her manipulation is evident when she pretends to mistake Elsa for Victor's daughter: "And you've brought Wendy! How lovely to meet you Wendy!" Gemma then goes on to mistake her for his wife, Janice, but Victor corrects her, saying, "This is Elsa; you asked me to bring her down. You know perfectly well" (7).

Both Victor and Elsa are enamored by the opulence of the estate, though it is clear that wealth has not made Hamish and Gemma happy people. Victor wants to take advantage of his rich friends by purchasing some of their antiques at a good price and by becoming Gemma's antique dealer. The young, naive Elsa "has not a penny to her name" (3), and her fascination with the older, more well-to-do characters makes her unaware of their motives. Victor is culpable because he wants to take advantage of the rich couple and because he prizes Elsa, his former secretary, for her youth and beauty. Hamish and Gemma, having hidden motives, use their power and wealth to entrap both Victor and Elsa, inviting them to the estate for reasons other than the antique enterprise.

The book depends on a variety of fairy tales for its structure. Elsa is the victim, the prey to other characters, the child who has left home to live with an older man. Shown to her room on the fourth floor, Elsa leans out of the window and "[h]er long hair falls over the sill and down over empty space. She is frightened" (8). Seeing a typewriter on a desk, which reminds her of her own poor typing skills, Elsa thinks "of the incompetent peasant girl who boasted of her prowess at weaving, and was shut up in the castle by the king and set to work weaving hanks of straw into gold, on pain of death. Has Elsa likewise claimed to be what she is not—a secretary, when in fact she can barely type a line without smudges and mistakes? Is her presumption now to be punished? And who is her Rumpelstiltskin to be, the dwarf who visits by night and performs the impossible task, claiming her first-born child unless she can guess his name?" (9). As it turns out, Hamish, a good typist, will visit her room at night to do the typing set out for her by Gemma. Further, he is the representative dwarf who in a perverse twist will try to claim her child, by the act of fathering it. The barren Gemma has plotted a sexual liaison between Elsa and Hamish so that she and Hamish can have the child. Neither Victor nor Elsa is aware of the couple's motives. At Victor's request, Elsa agrees to have sex with Hamish. Victor hopes this sacrifice will convince Hamish to lower his price on the antiques.

Gemma's narrative provides the background to her current, wealthy lifestyle with Hamish. As a young woman, she is the victim of wealth and power, losing her mother, who "died when Gemma was four, from (some said) too many late nights and too much rackety living, and (others said) from TB aggravated by self neglect" (22). Taken in by her arthritic great-aunt May, she lives with her until age 16, when her 70-year-old aunt put her "into the care of the local Children's Department" (23). Within a few weeks she takes employment with a vicar's wife, hired to take care of her five children. After two years and receiving a certificate in shorthand and typing from a correspondence school, Gemma leaves for London, where a secretarial agency sends her to a temp job with Fox and First, who make erotic jewelry. When she gets to the job a more homely woman, Marion, is responsible for the actual secretarial needs, and so Gemma, attractive, slim, and desirable, will model the jewelry. Immediately she falls in love with Fox, a more attractive man than First. Gemma, entrapped in a romantic myth, overlooks the potential danger of her new workplace. First's sister has recently jumped out of a window of a skyscraper (another tower), and when Marion tells the story, it seems that First is responsible. Someone, probably First, has cut off the sister's finger. Marion also suggests that the sister was in love with Fox. In spite of that foreboding story, Gemma remains enamored by her new employers, believing in the mythical salvation that Fox may afford her. Clearly, Gemma is, as Elsa will later be, caught in a fairy tale of her own creation. A self-made Cinderella, she waits, while ignoring the imminent dangers at Fox and First, for a hero to rescue her. Inexperienced and unworldly, she continues to dream of Fox, whose name suggests his predatory nature.

Marion asks Gemma to stay with her and her parents, the Ramsbottles. The parents and daughter have a combative relationship, the parents hinting that Marion is mad and threatening to send her back to a mental hospital. Rejecting Marion, they favor Gemma and her attempt to gain access to the power at Fox and First. Marion's homeliness and practicality lack the romance that her parents long for; her ability to see the perversion at Fox and First holds a truth that neither her parents nor Gemma wants to see. The Ramsbottles want to live in a myth, more attracted to Gemma because she is not in touch with reality. Marion's supposed madness, then, is a sham: she is the one who is aware of reality. Life is indeed perverse, replete with false saviors who prey on those whose idyllic views blind them to reality. Marion has not been completely honest with Gemma about the situation at Fox and First; in fact, she has the finger, the expensive ring still on it, of the sister in her chest of drawers. Marion is the caretaker of the perverse, the one who realizes that life is fraught with danger. Gemma, however, is seduced by the beautiful, by jewels—as her name suggests—and when Marion shows her the finger, Gemma removes the ring, putting it on her own finger. Unable to remove it she wears it to work, planning to have it removed during her lunch hour. When Fox sees the ring, he begins to chase her around the office with an ax, reminiscent of the severing of his sister's finger. Fox, as his name implies, is the dangerous one, not First, and is responsible for the death of First's sister. Marion, with the help of her parents, and First rescue Gemma but not before Fox chops off her finger. On the elevator after her rescue, Gemma falls in love with First, who turns out to be Hamish. Gemma's fairy tale, then, appears to end happily with a rescue by a prince of sorts. The fairy tale is illusory, however, and she will find herself paralyzed and miserable in her castle, creating a wicked tale of her own.

Once Gemma's tale ends we realize that her words of advice to Elsa reveal the danger of idealistic illusions that seduce the young and powerless. Gemma's story warns Elsa that she is at risk and that in an ironic twist, Gemma, a former victim, has become the predator. A rich woman now, the unhappy Gemma has devised the plan to steal Elsa's child. Although Elsa does not understand the significance of Gemma's fairy tale, it harbors a warning, if indeed she could interpret it, that she is the victim in the perverse fairy tale developing at the estate. A naive Elsa, though, remains vulnerable to the motives of those who would take advantage of her youth and beauty: to Victor, who is using her as a stopgap during his estrangement from his wife, and to Hamish and Gemma, who want her child.

Weldon uses the allegorical fairy tale to comment on women's position in the social power structure. Elsa, as victim, exemplifies the young woman, new to the world, valued in the larger world only for her body and youthfulness. As a secretary she becomes an easier target in the capitalist system of men who will exploit her. Gemma, having experienced the same victimization, has resorted to a predatory mode of survival. Now she preys on the powerless Elsa, who has entered her powerful domain, which she has established through a male power figure. Unable to bear children, Gemma represents the barren witch who in a social sense fails to fulfill the important role of mother. In a plot reminiscent of the tale of Hansel and Gretel, Gemma tries to steal children to acquire that lost power. Gemma's ambivalence toward her victim, however, couples cruelty with empathy. Her personal desire to have a child is complicated by another desire—to set Elsa free. Such a rewriting of the fairy tale provides a different vision to power structures. By letting Elsa go, Gemma is herself freed from her own ideological prison. The fairy tale is illusory but can only be transcended through an empathy that works counter to the myth.

Gemma's cruel methods come to fruition when, having invited Janice and Wendy to the estate, Victor leaves with his wife. Gemma has planned and predicted this ending, hoping to have Elsa remain with her and Hamish until the baby is born. The collapse of Gemma's fairy tale begins to occur, however, when Hamish points out some falsehoods in the narrative Gemma has shared with Elsa. He tells Gemma, for example, that her paralysis began after they were married. He says, "You have not walked since. There is no organic damage, the doctors say. Only an emotional disturbance for which you will accept no treatment" (210). In response to Hamish's words, Gemma admits that her story contains falsehoods: " 'One story or another, Hamish,' she says, 'what's the difference? It is all the same. It's the one-way journey we all make from ignorance to knowledge, from innocence to experience. We must all make it; there is no escape. It's just that love and romance and illusion and hope are etched so deeply into all our hearts that they can never quite be wiped away. They stay around to torment us with thoughts of what might have been. For you as well as me. We are fallen creatures; we never quite lost sight of grace, and the pain of our fall is always with us' " (210–11). In these lines Gemma finally speaks the truth: Gemma's psychosomatic paralysis is the result of trying to make life conform to romantic ideals. Yet Gemma is not ready to end her story. It is only when she identifies with her great-aunt May that she begins to relinquish her myth. Recognizing that her great-aunt May took her in to fend off death, she says: "That's why you did it. Yes, you did. That was the end you feared. You had no child of your own, so you stole your sister's daughter's child" (211). Gemma's desire for a child repeats her great-aunt May's pattern to fend off death, but her actions are far more venal than that of her great-aunt. She has taken the family history and twisted it, especially in her cruelty to Elsa. Fending off death through the acquisition of children may be a human impulse, but Gemma has taken it to a perverse extreme. When she tells Elsa that they will rear her child and that "you can go back to your typing pool, or wherever you're happy, six weeks after the birth," Great-Aunt May's voice intercedes as Gemma begins to speak to herself: " 'What are you saying?' " she asks, and her face is contorted, and an old-lady croak comes out of her mouth to match her old-lady face. 'You're being very naughty, Gemma.' Great-Aunt May's words, Great-Aunt May's voice. Great-Aunt May perhaps" (212).

Great-Aunt May's voice breaks the spell that Gemma has cast, and Gemma gives way to her empathy for Elsa: " 'Run, Elsa, run,' " says Gemma in her new, old cracked voice, herself transcended. " 'The door's open. Just run. Please run' " (212). This transcendence arises from Gemma's understanding that she must end the fairy tale of power and let the victim go free. When she cries "Run!" again, it is with her mother's voice yelling to Elsa to escape as once she had tried to do; thus, her words of advice speak to all women: "Run, Elsa! Run for all you're worth. Don't fall. Please don't fall, the way I did. You can do it; go so far and then draw back. I know you can. You must! You must run for me and all of us" (213). As Elsa runs for the gate, she turns to see Gemma walking, freed from the wheelchair, her figurative prison. When Gemma relinquishes her myth, she realizes that the oppression of other women for the sake of power allows the myth to survive. Women must identify with female suffering by breaking the model, by recognizing the urge to repeat the past. Using the allegorical fairy tale, Weldon portrays myths as psychological constructs that can be evaded and revisioned.

When Elsa reaches a phone booth, she calls her mother: "You were right. . . . Men are beasts.' " Her mother responds: "I never said they were beasts . . . just that you were a fool" (214). The novel ends, then, with some kindness toward the male characters. Men are beasts as long as innocent young women live in a romantic myth, ignoring the dangers of a world ruled by the powerful. Weldon rewrites the fairy tale for Elsa, allowing her to escape, but the author's warning is clear: to be a fool is to make oneself vulnerable in a world rife with those in search of a victim.

Chapter Four
Female Nature

Nature works by waste. Those that survive are indeed strong but not necessarily happy: Auntie Evolution, Mother Nature—bitches both! (*Puffball*, 101)

Biological determinants influence human behavior in Weldon's fiction. Inscribing her characters with universal innate tendencies, Weldon balances this view with one that considers the cultural interpretation of what is "natural." Biologically innate behaviors may exist, but how have they influenced our cultural conception of gender? she asks. Gender attributes easily lead to the justification and sanctioning of certain types of behavior. The idealization of the mothering instinct, for example, leads to economically powerless women who surrender their lives to husband and children in order to prove their natural inclinations. Certainly it is praiseworthy to protect and care for one's children, but this sentiment easily becomes propaganda for selling products. Gender stereotyping also feeds into sexist notions of the roles that women and men should play. *Praxis* and *Puffball* contemplate the concept of nature as it applies to women. The irony strikes at nature itself, though as well at the ideologically laden term. Women, she suggests, have defined what is natural to them according to slogans and precepts. In *Praxis* the central character becomes a writer for advertising, creating slogans that tell women, for example, "God made her a woman. . . . Love made her a mother—with a little help from electricity!" (196). What is the true nature of women? Weldon asks. *Puffball* celebrates motherhood, affirming female biology and the mystery of giving birth, while showing how mothering, too, can be self-serving.

Praxis

Praxis is narrated by the title character, Praxis, whose name means "turning point, culmination, action; orgasm; some said the Goddess herself" (12). Her story is a retrospective that begins in her childhood, in the 1920s. With her only sibling, a sister, Hypatia, she experiences a horrid childhood with unmarried parents, Ben and Lucy, whose brutal fights result in Ben's leaving Lucy and his daughters in an old house in Brighton. A substitute father, Henry Whitechapel, moves in with them for awhile but he, too, leaves, running off with the housekeeper, Judith. Soon after, the girls' mother goes insane and the girls are left to fend for themselves. In addition to Lucy's madness, Praxis must also deal with Hypatia's mental instability, explained to a degree in the origin of her name: "a learned woman; stoned to death by an irate crowd for teaching mathematics when she should have stayed modestly at home" (12). Hypatia's intelligence places her outside the prescriptive feminine roles of the era and she rebels by going mad. Praxis, on the other hand, "the pretty one" of the two, becomes the caretaker of both her sister and mother. The sisters' names, given to them by their father, are changed by their mother to more socially acceptable ones—Patricia and Hilda—when they enter elementary school.

The first-person narration of Praxis when she is an old woman, with her regrets and self-realizations, adds the texture of hindsight to a third-person narrative that follows Praxis from childhood to old age. Early in the novel the old Praxis explains the significance of her name and the importance of her journey to the new generation of women. Through her suffering Praxis brings this younger generation to a turning point, to a figurative and real orgasm. Through her experiences Praxis has discovered that the denial of female desire is at the root of female oppression. The female orgasm, then, is an act of liberation. Ironically, though, the old Praxis is shocked and somewhat appalled by the new generation of women: "The New Women! I could barely recognize them as being of the same sex as myself, their buttocks arrogant in tight jeans, openly inviting, breasts falling free and shameless, feeling no apparent obligation to smile, look pleasant or keep their voices low. And how they live! Just look at them to know how! If a man doesn't bring them to orgasm, they look for another who does. If by mistake they fall pregnant, they abort by vacuum aspiration" (16).

Praxis's philosophical insight also appears early in the retrospective as she describes the remorse of past actions especially in her treatment of her children: "Children who have been hurt grow up to hurt. This I know. I knew it but was helpless in the knowledge. I shouted and screamed, attempted murder or faced suicide, in my children's presence: conducted the dark side of my erotic nature beneath their startled gaze, careless of the precipice I opened up beneath their feet" (24). Praxis expresses the awful regrets that only a parent can feel, although she recognizes that the harm she has done to her children has arisen from the pain she has suffered at the hands of her own parents. She ponders her mother's actions, but her narrative also offers forgiveness to herself and others as she describes life's difficult choices and the complicated nature of human action.

When Patricia is 15 and Hilda 18, their mother is committed to a mental institution. A few months later Patricia is sent to live with Miss Leonard, an English teacher at her school, who becomes pregnant after a night on the town, having sex with three different men. Absurdly, she dies while giving birth, when a "London-aimed buzz bomb" landed inland. Her body is crushed but the baby, Mary, is saved by a woman who bites through the umbilical cord (74). The child is taken in by the local vicar and his wife.

Praxis leaves Brighton to attend Exeter University, quickly having her first sexual experience at a dance at which she gets drunk and is taken advantage of by two young men, Willie and Phillip. Outside on the downs, Phillip pushes her down on the ground and has sex with her while Willie objects. Though enamored of Phillip, Praxis begins a relationship with Willie, typing and correcting his college papers, neglecting her own studies in fear of his rejection. Playing the role of the dutiful girlfriend, Praxis surrenders to his sexual desires, receiving no pleasure in return: "[N]either he nor she herself seemed to expect a female response in the least equivalent to the male. She never cried out, or thought she should or knew that women did, or why they would" (91). This surrender of her body without expectation of physical pleasure reflects the unquestioned sexual attitudes of the period when a woman's singular purpose was to please rather than to be pleased. Female desire was not simply denied; it was undiscovered. In Praxis's journey of self-discovery, she acquiesces to the objectification of her body as men use her for their physical pleasure, but as she becomes more autonomous, she begins to understand that she, too, has sexual desires. Her attractiveness coupled with her intelligence complicates her journey because she finds advantage in using her appearance to gain favor with men, yet the necessity of hiding her intelligence is dissatisfying, leading her through numerous unfulfilling relationships as she tries to play the traditional feminine role. Praxis seeks the orgasm that will indeed turn her life around.

Praxis's relationship with Willie leads to one such orgasm, but she must first experience the rigors of discontent with Willie that characterize their lives together. He persuades her to return to Brighton and live in the old house on Holden Road. Giving up a college degree, she becomes a housewife and mother, having taken over responsibility for Baby Mary. Leading a boring, ineffectual life, her frustration leads to prostitution at a local bar where she and her friend from elementary school sell themselves to men during the day while Willie is at work. The fortuitous orgasm occurs while having sex with a man who turns out to be her father: "She cried out in genuine orgasm: she had all but forgotten how not to feign them" (129). She doesn't realize that the man is her father until after the encounter when he tells her he had been "more or less" married to Looney Lucy. Knowing that she is now willingly committing incest, she has sex with him again. Praxis's lack of repulsion in the act reminds us that our heroine is exploring the depths of her psyche and this Electra experience functions as a way for her to reject social conditioning to find her true self. Praxis leaves off self-loathing for action, and within a few hours she has left Willie and returned to London to her friend Colleen's house. In the taboo scene, Praxis has had the opportunity not only to meet a father who has deserted her but to know him in the most intimate way.

That incestuous experience allows Praxis to move forward in her life, but her escape from Willie does not lead to more satisfying relationships with men. She has two more marriages, one with Ivor, a production manager at a soup mix firm with whom she has two children. They live together in the suburbs of London in new executive estates. She finds life there stultifying; looking at herself in the mirror she sees "her doll's face, stiff doll's body, curly blonde doll's hair" (168). Her friend Irma, now married to Phillip, calls Praxis one day and asks her to tend to the household while she gives birth to another baby. Praxis takes the opportunity to leave Ivor and her children, sleeping with Phillip and eventually marrying him. Irma becomes a women's libber and tries to persuade Praxis to follow in kind. Praxis holds out, however, until, again miserable in her marriage with Phillip, she finds him in bed with another woman. Soon she becomes a convert and begins to work on a "weekly broadsheet, devoted to the wrongs done to women by society" (232). The most significant turning point comes when Praxis murders Baby Mary's mongoloid infant, suffocating him with a pillow while Mary is out of the room. After serving two years in prison, Praxis moves to a basement apartment where she relates her story. In an interview Weldon explains that "Praxis is a Victorian girl's name; it also means orgasm and for a Marxist it's the moment when theory takes actual practical form. You could say that Praxis' smothering of the mongoloid baby is the turning-point, it's the culmination of everything these women have gone through in our society. Praxis wanted to liberate her step-daughter Mary, who otherwise would be put into a lifetime's servitude by her loving female nature. *Praxis* is a fictionalised working-out of all the meanings of that word, through the trends in our society which make women victims."[1]

The two most transformative events in Praxis's life are taboo: incest and infanticide. These symbolic acts bring the deeper, darker side of human consciousness to the surface, questioning what is natural and what is hidden. Women have been conditioned to feel guilty about sex and to sacrifice themselves for their children. Praxis, by the end of the novel, does neither, an antiheroine who not only rejects conventional roles but acts in ways that deny all concepts of the feminine ideal. These extreme examples examine the codes of correct behavior. The primal has been all but erased in women, yet it lies beneath layers of social conditioning. In Praxis's behavior Weldon undoes the cultural notion of women as pure and sacrificial. To sacrifice oneself for children while ignoring one's own sexual needs is natural according to social definition. But Praxis comes to realize that "Nature does not know best; for the birds, for the bees, for the cows; for men, perhaps. But your interests and Nature's do not coincide. Nature our Friend is an argument used, quite understandably, by men" (133).

Praxis further considers the meaning of the word *natural* when she reflects upon having left her children. In social terms motherhood is natural, thus to deny this role amounts to a crime against nature: "When I was young it was rare for a mother to leave her children. It was considered an unspeakable thing to do—an unnatural crime" (177). Though Praxis expresses sympathy for her children and all children to whom the world is "a dangerous place," she offers no apologies for leaving them. In justification she says, "I think perhaps if you want to leave a child, if you cannot love it, you should leave it before the look in your eye shrivels its life and its hopes" (178). Of course, Praxis does not wholly abandon her children to an uncertain future but leaves them with the men who she believes will care for them. Baby Mary, for example, stays with Willie, who treats her as his own daughter.

When Praxis smothers the mongoloid baby, she frees Mary from self-sacrifice to the child whose condition is "very low-grade. . . . He will sit in a chair and dribble and wear nappies when he's a grown man" (214). Further, Mary will be able to return to her career as a doctor. By killing the baby, Praxis has enacted a symbolic turning point for all women, freeing them to pursue independent, self-fulfilling lives. Praxis's name embodies the novel's feminist message. Women must take action to bring about their own liberation—their figurative orgasm will only occur when they surrender passive, self-effacing roles and pursue their own destinies.

Puffball

In *Puffball*, the main character, Liffey, has persuaded her husband, Richard, to move from London to Somerset, a village 20 miles away. Because of the difficulties of commuting to his job in London, Richard resides with friends there, visiting the cottage on the weekends. The natural setting in the novel is ominous; nature is not bucolic and peaceful but frightening, a place where the unnatural occurs. Down the road, a country pair, Tucker and Mab, represent the quaint simplicity of country life, raising cattle, living quite simply, lacking intellect, and duly threatened by their new neighbors. The two are caricatures of country folk who view the city couple as a threat. Practically, they want the couple to rent the cottage because they are using the pasture from the cottage for their cattle. If the property is sold, then they will have to give up this portion of land on the other side of the creek to the new owner. The earthy Mab, however, finds Liffey's thinness and delicacy a threat, using potions and spells to bring harm to her unsuspecting neighbor.

Puffball literally refers to mushrooms around the cottage, but symbolically refers to the novel's main theme—pregnancy. Weldon has said that "I wanted to nail down what it feels like to be pregnant. And writing a novel is a similar creative process".[1] Liffey becomes pregnant during the course of the novel, and Mab wants to become pregnant, though she despises her children. Her mythical naming also refers to the Welsh word for baby—*Mab*. Cows also function as important figures, their fatness and complacency comically reflect pregnancy or fertility. When Tucker makes love to Mab he "loved the way her sharp brown eyes, in the act of love, turned soft and docile, large-irised, like those of cows" (13). Procreation is associated with fullness in the novel: the cow and the fat mushroom images represent the pregnant female body, a distorted image that Weldon treats as a kind of aberration rather than a sweet portrait of womanhood. With all of Mab's tricks, her teas and soups that contain potions, Liffey's baby prevails. As it grows in the womb, the child is a silent half-character in the novel, the narrative intermittently returning to the interior of Liffey's body via subtitles "Inside Liffey": "By Saturday morning the fine hairs of the blastocyst inside Liffey had digested and eroded enough of the uterus wall to enable it to burrow snugly into the endometrium and there open up another maternal blood vessel, the better to obtain the oxygen and nutrients it increasingly required" (112). This narrative technique reveals the hidden world of the womb, nature at work, which is more or less unconscious for the mother. Though Liffey begins to address the child, what goes on in the womb is mysterious, what the child experiences unknown. Passages describing the growth of the child, abundant in factual detail, continue until the child's birth: the mechanics of nature follow an ancient logic of survival. Olga Kenyon says that the novel "*dignifies* female experience by incorporating scientific language to tell a wide public about the growing foetus and the hormonal effects on a woman's mind. Never before has the struggle between reason and unreason, triggered by pregnancy, been so sympathetically and *dramatically* detailed" (Kenyon, 119).

Before Liffey becomes pregnant, the narrative takes us inside her body to the routine of ovulation, the activity of hormones, the menstrual flow with its excretion of the uterus lining. There is an "Outer Liffey, with her fluttery smiley eyes, sweet curvy face, dark curly hair and white smooth skin. And there was an inner Liffey, cosmic Liffey, hormones buzzing, heart beating, blood surging, pawn in nature's game" (15). This silent world of nature continues to follow its genetic plan as Liffey moves through the outside world of human experience unaware of this inner world that nonetheless influences her actions. When the baby begins to speak to her, Liffey finds a link between the outer and inner self and becomes more self-protective in an effort to protect the child within.

Mab's first trick is to spike Liffey's elderberry wine with an herb that makes her feel sexual. She sends Tucker to visit, and helpless to resist, Liffey has sex with him. This ploy is carried out in an effort to subdue Liffey, to show her to be "the slut she is." Living in a world of sexual reproduction, raising cows for profit, children for self-gratification, Mab uses sexual prowess, through her submissive husband, to try to control Liffey. In another example, she tries to unsettle the pregnant Liffey by insisting that she observe the birthing of a cow: "The calf was dead when Mabs pulled it out by its emergent leg, tugging and grunting, while the cow lowed and moaned. When the calf's head came out, it was putrid—pulpy and liqueous. Then the cow heaved and groaned and died" (131). The unscrupulous Mab is frightening, and Weldon succeeds in making us wonder whether she will destroy Liffey and her baby, but with a charming turn Weldon allows the baby a knowledge that the mother doesn't have: " 'It's me,' said the spirit, said the baby, 'I'm here. I have arrived. You are perfectly all right and so am I. Don't worry' " (127–28). From this point, Mab's efforts to destroy the mother and child are thwarted as Liffey begins to realize that Mab is not a kindly neighbor but a dark force. Tucker, too, the pawn of his wife, becomes protective of Liffey and warns her to avoid the wine that Mab so willingly provides.

Though Richard is the father of her child, Liffey feels guilty about her infidelity, fearing that Tucker may be the father. Yet Richard, remaining in London, has sexually betrayed her with numerous women. In considering his betrayals, Richard blames his wife: for her desire to move to the country, and for other mistakes. Liffey's guilt for her indiscretion is in contrast to her husband's willing, petulant betrayals. Richard increasingly justifies his sexual exploits and at one point categorizes the women as types who fulfill him in different ways. Liffey he views as the dutiful wife; Bella, the sexually experimental, hungry partner; and Miss Martin, the emotionally vulnerable woman he can manipulate. He concludes: "It would not be possible, nor indeed desirable . . . to find these three different women in one body; he could never satisfy his needs monogamously. Could any man?" (108). As is usual for Weldon's men, Richard gives reason to his philandering whereas Liffey values her marriage and tries to suppress sexual desire other than that for her husband. Neither attitude is necessarily correct; monogamy seems more social than natural in Weldon's fiction. What does come through as nature's plan is Liffey's desire to give birth to a healthy child and provide it with a nurturing home.

Convinced that Liffey's baby is fathered by Tucker, Mab feels that her neighbor has stolen the child from her. Although she abuses and ignores her children, she loves being pregnant. Failing to become pregnant herself, Mab grows more and more angry toward Liffey, sticking pins in wax dolls made in the baby's image and spiking the food and drink she gives Liffey. Mab's witchiness and the viability of her spells are contrivances that allow Weldon to probe evil motives against the backdrop of biological destiny. The desire to reproduce may be natural, but psychology brings individual perspectives to the role of parenting. Mab is the twisted version of the mother whose love of pregnancy is an obsession with her own potency. She is, in fact, a kind of aberration of nature, as evidenced in her cruelty to her children. Mab's perverse mothering puts into question the concept of *natural,* suggesting that women too can be cruel and that, obversely, men, like her husband, Tucker, who cares for his children, can be nurturers.

Mab's final attempt to destroy Liffey and her baby occurs when she invites the couple to dinner and reveals that Tucker may be the father. " 'Thief,' " she cried. 'You stole what was mine. I hope you die' " (224). Richard rushes out, returning to London, and Tucker, too, leaves in the car. When Liffey begins to bleed, Mab tears the telephone from the wall and Liffey can do nothing but walk down the road guided by Mab and Tucker's half-wit son, Eddie, until she is rescued by the doctor, who takes her to the hospital where she gives birth to Baby Lee-Fox. Mab follows her there but upon seeing the infant laughs at how much he resembles his father, Richard. Knowing that Liffey has not stolen Tucker's child from her, she leaves and conceives with her husband. Happily, the novel ends with Richard returning to the cottage and carrying an armful of toys and stuffed animals, accepted by the baby, who "smiled at Richard too, claiming him for father, shuffler of the genes. Liffey knew that that was that. The baby claimed them all, everyone, as bit-part players in his drama, dancers in his dance, singers to his tune" (248).

Chapter Five

Myths of Romance
and Domestic Life

Mary Fisher lives in a High Tower, on the edge of the sea: she writes a great deal about the nature of love. She tells lies. (*The Life and Loves of a She-Devil*, 1)

The President's Child, The Life and Loves of a She-Devil, and *The Leader of the Band* show the potentially harmful effects of romantic love when it becomes the sole source of pleasure and purpose for women. The novels' protagonists become immersed in the fantasy of romantic love ensconced in cultural myths, which gives them self-definition. Caught up in the love story, they surrender their identities to live in a world of illusion: "That romantic love is the source of both pleasure and oppression for women is a theme that runs through Weldon's novels" (Hebert, 22). In *The President's Child,* Isabel's absorption in the myth puts her in danger from her former lover, a powerful man who is running for president of the United States. Ruth in *The Life and Loves of a She-Devil* re-creates her body in the image of Mary Fisher, a romance writer who has taken away Ruth's husband. Envious of Mary, Ruth creates her own perverse love story wherein she becomes the romantic heroine. Sandra of *Leader of the Band* lives in a dream world, infatuated by a trumpet player, her "knight in shining armour" (14). Isabel and Sandra have realizations that help them escape their myths, but Ruth, though victorious in usurping Mary, creates a love story that, in effect, destroys her identity.

The President's Child

The President's Child is structured as a suspense novel with Isabel in danger from a former lover, Dandy Ivel, who is running for president of the United States. Some seven years back she had an affair with Dandy when he was a U.S. senator, sharing several weeks of passion with him in a hotel in Georgetown, where they fall in love. His political strategists, however, plan for Dandy to run for the presidency, and they see Isabel as a threat to this accession. Through their manipulation, the couple part, with Isabel escaping one night to return to England. On the plane home, she meets her husband, Homer. Pregnant with Dandy's child, she lets Homer believe he is the father. Nonetheless, Ivel's political strategists view Isabel's place in Dandy's life as a threat, and they keep surveillance on her to measure the degree of harm she could cause him. Eventually, with Dandy's approval, they plot to kill her.

The novel's narrative moves between a first-person narrator, Maia, a blind woman who lives in Isabel's neighborhood, and the third-person narration, which carries the suspense. Maia comments on the condition of the women's lives around her and is the confidante of her female neighbors. When running away from an argument with her husband, Maia is hit by a car and blinded. The blindness, though, is psychosomatic and in her self-chosen darkness, Maia's vision is keen. Maia's commentary on the social positioning of women is less severe than commentary in Weldon's early novels, carrying a softer, philosophical tone. There are fewer direct insults to patriarchal dominance and more contemplative musings about human relationships.

Isabel's story of her love affair with Dandy is told as a confessional to a psychologist, Dr. Gregory. Hired to treat Isabel's son, Jason, he implies that something is hidden in the family, something that disturbs the child. Isabel tells the doctor about her relationship with Dandy, describing the affair by using the language of mythos—of religion and fantasy. She "took on the lineaments of the divine" worshiped by Dandy. Their sexual unification is mystical and "the twisting of the body on the horrific pin of perverse desires—is purification" (93). Another form of ideology, politics, undermines their "state of grace" (100), and Isabel is chased away by Dandy's advisers.

Isabel's participation and creation of the romantic scenario involve her in her own potential destruction. The falsehoods inherent in the love relationship blind her to the powerful forces that try to destroy her. The novel suggests that women have only two places in the political structure: that of advancing or inhibiting the political careers of men. Women who can advance the cause of men, such as Dandy's fiancée, are tolerated for their ability to help the politician win. Women such as Isabel are allowed to please men sexually but cannot exist in the world of hype and media that brings men to power. Children, too, are at risk because they bear witness to the sexual indiscretions that may ruin the aspirations of the man seeking political office. Isabel expresses this idea to Maia: "[W]hen male power and prestige are at stake the lives and happiness of women and children are immaterial" (163). Referring to the novel as a political allegory, Weldon has said that "[i]t's also about the impossibility of pretending that there isn't a conflict between male power and female power" (Haffenden, 307–8).

The conspiracy to kill Isabel involves all the significant men in her life as they all work for Dandy's henchmen, including her husband, her psychiatrist, and her boss. In her last visit to Dr. Gregory's office she finds Homer there. The two inform her that she must sacrifice her life for Jason, who is having ice cream with Joe and Pete in a café outside the building. She agrees to follow their instructions to walk into the traffic-busy street below, but when she gets there, she crosses without harm to where Jason is waiting. Strangely, Joe and Pete are gone and a waitress tells her that Dandy Ivel has died. Isabel returns home and tells her story to Maia, who miraculously regains her vision. Thus, the blindness brought about by immersion in the fantasy of romance exemplified in Isabel's intriguing story has been paralleled by Maia's blind narrative. When Maia hears Isabel's story, she realizes that "[t]here is no pure and perfect victory for Good" (230), and in a "fit of despair" regains her sight (231). The story of power, then, brings revelation to Isabel and Maia. The novel insists on seeing, rather than being blinded by romantic fantasies.

The Life and Loves of a She-Devil

The Life and Loves of a She-Devil is Weldon's best-known novel, having been made into a Hollywood movie starring Rosanne Barr and Meryl Streep. The movie failed to capture the hard-hitting satiric quality of the novel or its quirky sci-fi, horror plot. Weldon, quoting Oscar Wilde, has said about the movie that "[i]t reminded me vaguely of something I once wrote."[1] The novel is a fantastic tale that combines science fiction, horror, and a perverse fairy tale. Weldon satirizes the modern concept of romance, rendering an absurd vision of the physically ideal woman. The central characters are two opposing figures: Ruth, the ugly, undesirable woman whose husband has been stolen away by Mary Fisher, a romance writer and perfect rendition of femininity. When Ruth's husband, Bobbo, leaves her for Mary, Ruth retaliates out of hatred and vengeance. Treated poorly her entire life, she enacts a plot that ruins both her husband's and Mary's life. Ruth describes herself: "I am six feet two inches tall, which is fine for a man but not for a woman. I am as dark as Mary Fisher is fair, and have one of those jutting jaws that tall, dark women often have, and eyes sunk rather far back into my face, and a hooked nose. My shoulders are broad and bony and my hips broad and fleshy, and the muscles in my legs are well developed. My arms, I swear, are too short for my body. My nature and my looks do not agree. I was unlucky, you might think, in the great lottery that is woman's life" (5).

The story is an uncanny rewriting of the Pygmalion myth, with Ruth hiring doctors to physically remake her in the image of Mary. Ruth's self-restructuring, however, is purely physical; she understands that social acceptance lies in appearance and that lacking beauty, she cannot change her effect on people by simply changing her behavior. She in fact realizes that she is repugnant, lacking all physical qualities of the feminine, in contrast to Mary Fisher, who is "small and pretty and delicately formed, prone to fainting and weeping and sleeping with men while pretending that she doesn't" (2). *The Life and Loves of a She-Devil* also parodies two other myths of transformation and creation: Frankenstein and the ugly duckling. In Weldon's revision of these tales, women, no longer the sub-sidiaries in the drama, become the creators. Of course, Ruth's self-recon-struction ironically agrees with the notion of the culturally feminine, ful-filling the social image that has been the source of her self-denigration and alienation. She embraces the romantic myth by attempting to usurp Mary Fisher's place in order to find recognition and adoration. Ann Marie Hebert notes that "The body, the primary locus of patriarchal control over women, serves as both the reality and the metaphor of women's oppression in Weldon's novels. From Esther's eating disorder to Ruth's self-mutilating cosmetic surgery, the female protagonists try to exercise control over 'nature' by exercising control over their bodies" (Hebert, 30).

Establishing Ruth's nemesis as a writer of popular romance novels, Weldon shows how power is embedded in cultural ideology. While Mary enjoys a blessed life in her tower because of her beauty and ability to capture audiences with romantic scenarios, Ruth languishes in a middle-class suburb, with two children, a dog, a cat and a guinea pig, sub-servient to a husband who does not love her. Mary lives in a world of fantasy, producing romantic fiction that lies about the nature of mar-riage and love. Until Bobbo leaves, Ruth has been a good wife, obedient and long-suffering, derided by her husband for her clumsiness and lack of beauty. When Bobbo moves in with Mary, however, Ruth forswears her wifely goodness and resolves to change her nature by becoming the she-devil that Bobbo has accused her of being, swearing allegiance to hatred and vengeance: "I want revenge. I want power. I want money. I want to be loved and not love in return" (43). She begins her new role by burning her house and taking the children to the tower to live with Mary and Bobbo. She then disappears, plotting the destruction of Mary's idyllic life, which Mary now shares with Ruth's husband. The presence of the children in the tower brings the first taste of reality to Mary's world, causing disturbances in the household. "The children pressed dirty palms against snowy surfaces and kicked footballs against shiny glass and sprawled over the backs of sofas, breaking them, and stretched quilts to make trampolines, and tripped and sent family heirlooms flying. Andy, trying to play polo from the back of a Doberman, sent Mary Fisher's great-uncle's grandfather clock crashing to the ground. Mary Fisher wept."

Ruth defines her she-devil role as one of heartlessness and coldness, as evidenced in abandoning her children. To gain power she must empty herself of empathy and be willing to use people for her own selfish designs. Having been ruined by the cruelty of others, she ruthlessly adopts the same approach to gain privilege in a world that has marginalized her for being an ugly duckling. True to the fairy tale, Ruth decides to become the ugly duckling who changes into a swan, creating her own destiny. In contrast to Esther of *. . . And the Wife Ran Away,* who defies social standards by increasing her physical repulsiveness, Ruth aspires to achieve the feminine ideal through whatever means necessary. Ruth's decision reflects the social power structure and is motivated by egoism and disregard for others. The acquisition of power and money precludes concern for others and is valued above human compassion. When Ruth appropriates these solipsistic values, she adopts the ideology of a culture inured to beauty, fame, and money, colluding in her own oppression, as Patricia Waugh explains: "Weldon presents a heroine who believes she has broken free from the dominant economic and social structures of power, yet who uses her freedom in the pursuit of a romantic myth which continues to oppress her as effectively as purely economic constraints" (Waugh, 190).

To take control of her destiny and become the she-devil, Ruth must give up her faith in God: "I will be what I want, not what He ordained. I will mold a new image for myself out of the earth of my creation. I will defy my Maker, and remake myself" (162). As Frankenstein and monster, Ruth plans to have her body refashioned, through elaborate plastic surgery, to look like Mary Fisher's. Becoming beautiful on the outside, Ruth's nature and actions have become monstrous. She acquires the money for the expensive surgery by establishing a temporary secretarial service, gaining access to Bobbo's financial records through a temp whom she has placed in his office. Gradually, she transfers money from his customers' accounts, stealing several million dollars, which she deposits in a Swiss bank account. Bobbo, blamed for the extortion, ends up in jail, sequestered from his adoring lover, Mary. Through other contrivances Ruth manages to have Mary's elderly mother move to the tower and a judge to give Bobbo a seven-year sentence. Having brought misery to Mary and Bobbo, Ruth then begins the surgery that will re-create her in the image of Mary.

Ruth endures months of grueling surgery to change her face, having her jaw, teeth, and forehead modified, changes that are accomplished with ease in comparison to having her height reduced by removing inches from her legs. The doctors take satisfaction in remaking Ruth, but they balk at reducing her height, a procedure that has never been done. With her insistence, though, they proceed and she, at 5' 4", experiences great pain when walking. Ruth insists on being shorter than men, understanding that men find women who are shorter than they are to be more attractive. When the doctor asks Ruth what she wants, she tells him: " 'I want to look up to men' " (177). This line alludes to Freud's question of what women want, offering a comical answer that would flatter men. In fact, Ruth simply wants to be loved and understands that she must give the appearance of subservience by becoming shorter in order to evoke the response she desires. Ruth's hyperbolic reconstruction satirizes the abundant types of plastic surgery that women undergo to become more desirable. Physical augmentation in Weldon's novels is pointedly absurd, based on a desire to please men, an expression of self-hatred in the woman attempting to change herself to create a more socially pleasing image.

Ruth's misguided, macabre exercise of self-reconstruction has the effect, on the narrative level, of structurally undermining the myth of romantic love that seduces women. For Weldon this fantasy has become the modern equivalent of a fairy tale in modern romance novels. When Ruth destroys Mary's world, she shows her the realities of love that she has endured—loss, disappointment, and failure. Mary's chimeric fiction further denies the contingent nature of reality, the unsettling chaos that informs human existence. It is the philosophical equivocation of Mary's novels that Ruth most detests: "Mary Fisher did a wicked thing: she set herself up in a high building on the edge of a high cliff and sent a new light beaming out into the darkness. The light was treacherous; it spoke of clear water and faith and life when in fact there were rocks and dark and storms out there, and even death, and mariners should not be lulled but must be warned" (183). These lines can be read as a critique of contemporary fiction. Like Iris Murdoch's analysis of modernist fiction in which Murdoch criticizes the novelist who consoles the reader by indulging in fantasy,[2] Weldon's novel suggests that authors should not lull their readers with stories that ignore life's dangers or human mortality. Weldon, like Murdoch, does not believe in deceiving her audience, and Mary Fisher exemplifies the writer who doles out pablum to her readers, thus failing to warn them of the complexities of life's random events. The light coming from her tower shows only the glamorous, fortuitous possibilities of life, failing to show the darker events The parodic treatment of romantic myth in *The Life and Loves of a She-Devil* is echoed in other Weldon novels in which myth has entrapped the female characters, blinding them to the dangers of reality.

As Ruth strategically introduces real-life events to bring down Mary from her tower of privilege, the writer loses her ability to write successful fiction. With two children and an elderly mother in the tower and with Bobbo in jail, Mary is unable to write books with popular appeal. Mary's death by cancer leaves the tower empty and available for Ruth's occupation. In the protagonist's final major operation, to have her legs reduced, an electrical storm occurs and the doctor tells her that she has angered God. She replies, " 'Of course He's angry. . . . I am remaking myself ' " (234). Reminiscent of Frankenstein's creation of life, Ruth as she-devil defies God in order to bring her re-creation to fruition. Ruth finally finds the power over others she has been seeking. In the tower she takes Mary's servant lover as her own, and when Bobbo, confused and weakened, returns there to live with her, she "causes him as much misery as he ever caused me, and more. I try not to, but somehow it is not a matter of male or female, after all; it never was: merely of power. I have all, and he has none. As I was, so he is now" (241).

In the end Ruth has all that she has wanted—power, money, revenge, and love received without being returned. It is difficult to view Ruth's outcome as victorious, however. To maintain her power and control of others, she effectively loses her own humanity to gain possession of the tower. Being a she-devil is a lonely proposition and requires insensitivity to the suffering of others. There is some gratification in the novel's ending, however, to see the downtrodden, unfortunate Ruth granted a valued place in the social order. Yet Ruth's attainment of privilege has come about through her own self-destruction and heartlessness to others, not a fortuitous outcome in Weldon's fictional world.

Elisabeth Bronfen offers the following analysis of Ruth's outcome: "[T]he act of realizing her deep-seated desire for destruction is a sword that cuts both ways. Ruth has gained power by having resubstantiated an image. But this acquisition of power required that she deform herself into the image of perfect feminine beauty. . . . The impasse her excessive performance enacts is that in order to castrate her husband, and with the cultural formations he represents, she has to castrate herself, to die socially and somatically" (Barreca, 81).

The Leader of the Band

The Leader of the Band relates the escapades of another runaway wife in the weeks following her escape from her husband, Matthew. Starlady Sandra, an astronomer who has recently discovered a new planet, Athena, leaves with Jack, a trumpet player performing at a dinner party at her home. Hiding her true occupation and fame, she goes on the road with the band and its entourage, letting them (including Jack) believe she is a secretary. Living in a van, the group leaves for France where they are booked to play at a folk festival.

Sandra also hosts a TV program entitled *Sandra's Sky* in which she makes the science of astronomy accessible to the public. As not only a famed professional astronomer who has discovered a planet but also as a media celebrity, Sandra's star status becomes the book's central pun. When she tells a friend that Jack has proposed marriage, the friend responds, " 'Well, well! Aren't you lucky. Not many men will marry a star' " (68). Sandra understands that a successful woman is at a disadvantage when seeking love and companionship with men, thus she attempts to diminish her achievements when Jack discovers who she really is. She fears that her fame, financial success, and intelligence will threaten her relationship with Jack, and so she tries to appear common, grounded, if you will, rather than skybound where he and others must look up to her. A woman's desire for love is confounded by her stellar accomplishments; men in fact prefer women who are servile and who find meaning in their partners' aspirations and careers. Jennifer, one of the band members' wives, exemplifies this female type who is tolerated for her service to the group, cleaning the van and generally taking care of the group's needs. At one point Sandra asks, "Why do these men . . . always choose women less quick in the mind than they? (To say 'more stupid' would be unkind.) The answer, I daresay, is that only such women are prepared to rush after them proffering Brasso and cloth" (72).

Through Sandra's desperate desire for Jack's love, she compromises her own identity, following the path of self-dismissal to hold on to her companion. Her desire to be loved is expressed in her sexual longing for Jack, which gives her a false feeling of attachment. He represents the sexually attractive band member who is irresistible to women. She refers to him as her "knight in shining armour," says that she will "follow Jack Stubbs to the end of the earth," and also states, "If I can only hold my tongue I might yet be the one he keeps in his bed, for ever. Craven, yes indeed, but there it is. My female lost to his male. I love him. It's hopeless" (14). In this example Sandra uses the language of romantic sentiment to describe her willingness to surrender her identity to possess a man. Here Weldon lampoons the woman falling in love with an idea, with the band member who becomes an idealized notion of manhood.

Yet Weldon has, in Sandra, created a female character whose intelligence and independence play a significant part in her identity, although her subservience to Jack expresses an underlying need for love. Sandra is aware of these two conflicting elements of her personality and her loyalties are split; she is unlike many of Weldon's female protagonists who simply adopt the prescribed roles of women and the romantic myth with little awareness of their motives and actions. Sandra's thoughts contradict her actions—she understands, unlike some other Weldon protagonists, that her behavior clearly arises from social prescriptions. She is in the middle of a dilemma: her awareness is in conflict with her need to be loved. This ambivalence makes her a compelling character whose interior life allows her to be more representative of the vagaries of human existence and less a caricature or symbolic character.

Sandra's sexual passion for Jack embodies her conflicting feelings. Sex with Jack quells her self-doubts, yet she seeks sexual satisfaction for herself in ways that are typically identified with men. Realizing she will not have sex with Jack one morning, she says: "And so ended my hopes of at least some kind of sexual entendre with Jack before the day began. I like being woken in the morning by the thrust of the male member, before the mind is up and working, and the parts are swollen and stiff outside, but responsive and willing within, so orgasm comes suddenly and unexpectedly, taking the body quite by surprise" (12). Sandra's sexual desire, then, is not wholly to please but also to take pleasure for herself. These contrary feelings are commingled though in her desire for Jack. When he leaves her behind that same morning, she "feels a kind of lonely shuttered desolation." In response she masturbates on the door handle and "came and came again, and cried out without shame" (29). In this sexual act with the doorknob, she finds gratification, yet her desire arises from a feeling of loneliness. All the same, Sandra is embarrassed neither by her sexual longing nor the remedy for it: "My flesh and cold metal had had business together and very right it seemed. Thank you, long Jack. Thank you. Brass door handle. May the electrons fly, may the cells of the flesh learn how to welcome them, and not resist them" (29).

Sandra's life story explains to some extent her actions. Her father, a Nazi scientist, used his sperm to impregnate her gypsy mother and other women in a German work-camp laboratory. Abused by her schizophrenic mother, Sandra also has a mad brother, Robin, who commits suicide. This bizarre family history invades her thoughts, and she wonders at times whether she is mad. In fact, she is haunted by the ghost of her brother and another uncertain ghost that follows her. The haunting, though figurative, points to her need for love and may also explain her attraction for the blond Jack, who resembles her sadistic Aryan father, whose looks she has inherited. Sandra represents not only the victimized, her gypsy mother, the oppressed who were cruelly treated during the war, but also the awful sadist, her father, who perpetuated such acts. She finds in herself both victim and victimizer, troubled especially by her father's shadow: "I find myself thinking like my father, the Nazi beast. That is what happens when the work machine gets turned off: you find out who you are, how nasty you can be" (82). This coupling of mother and father within her creates confusion, but she identifies more with her father, finding herself to be more evil than good. Here is where Weldon takes the metaphor of good versus evil, monster versus victim, and places it within the realm of female experience. Sandra identifies with her terrible father rather than surrender to the madness of her mother. That may explain why Sandra at times seems cruel in her view of history. She wants, it seems, to defend her father, whom she never knew, perhaps to explain her own actions, attempting to adopt his views to give meaning to her own life. In reference to William Styron's novel *Sophie's Choice,* in which Sophie is given a choice by a Nazi officer to choose one of her children to live, Sandra says: "Why didn't she just grit her teeth and get on with it, or kill herself and both children with the materials at hand if she couldn't bear it? Moan, moan, moan, Sophie! I'm my father's daughter and have eliminated my own children in my time, and paid the man who held the scalpel very well to do it. That too was to perfect the race, by keeping my father's seed out of it" (105–6). Sandra contradicts herself here, practicing the cruelty of her father but admitting that she doesn't want to procreate to continue the genetic inheritance that she has been given.

Yet the gypsy side of her is expressed in her adventure with the gypsy-musician, and her travel with him is a metaphorical journey. Her wanderings are an escape from the part of herself that she associates with her father—prestige, beauty, power. Seeking anonymity, she lowers herself, identifying with those who choose to live outside the mainstream of society, trying to live like those of her mother's ancestors who were the victims of her father. Of course the real journey differs greatly from the historical one, and she is not like her ancestors though she tries to disenfranchise herself, seeking rootlessness and marginality. In fact much of Sandra's philosophical musings refer to genetics as she tries to come to terms with a father who tried to create a superior race and a mother who came from one that was punished for its dark color. She frequently refers to the randomness of genetic production. Comparing her own good looks with her brother's madness, she ponders the arbitrary nature of genetic inheritance. She refers to her own birth as abnormal, which leads her to make a comparison to the freewheeling operations of laboratory birth interventions: "Whipping out eggs by the dozen and fertilising a few and replanting them, and selectively terminating, or freezing the rest for later: surrogate mothers, and test tube babies, and other blessings. Thank you, Father, first in the field!" (106–7).

Like Esther in *. . . And the Wife Ran Away,* Sandra too returns to her former life when Jack's wife comes to join the group, though Sandra will not return to her husband, who wants a divorce and plans to marry Sandra's boss from the TV station. Discovering that she is pregnant, and contrary to all her former claims in which she forswears childbearing, Sandra decides to have the child. Her decision then is based on the affirmation of family life, that which she has never had. Thus, Sandra who has had meager experience of love and who has claimed the coldheartedness of her father and has troubled over having inherited the madness of her mother is, in the end, kind. Speaking with defiance and irreverence she makes her choice: "Let us pray! Great Father, Cruel God, simulator of the Universe, in whose image I am made, etc.? No, better not: no help there, God the Bastard! What the hell, Daddy-oh! I shall have this baby, even though it looks at me with your cold blue eyes" (155). In the end Sandra expresses faith in some human potential that transcends genetics. By having the baby she lets go of her identification with an evil father and perhaps with a mad mother.

The appendixes at the end of the novel are a collection of three stories written by Sandra about some of the novel's female characters, her friends Allison, Jude, and Jennifer. These appear without connection to Sandra's story, demonstrating her compassion for and understanding of female experience. Experimenting with form, Weldon attaches these stories as Sandra's interpretations, giving depth to characters whose lives have not been explored in the primary narrative. These multiple per-spectives remain true to Weldon's recapitulation of different points of view. They also point to how easily fiction manipulates the reader's atti-tude toward character by limiting the frame within which we view them. And they demonstrate that Sandra is more thoughtful and sensi-tive than she has purported and that her own suffering is not dissimilar to that of other women.

Chapter Six
Social Criticism

Nothing much to fear from radiation, compared to other dangers, compared to crossing the road, compared to smoking. A burst of intense radiation could kill you, sure. So could an overdose of aspirin. (*The Cloning of Joanna May*, 117)

Weldon's critique of the empowered begins in her novels of the late '80s and early '90s to encompass the derailed condition of postmodern culture; science, technology, and capitalism are her targets. Domestic and romantic scenarios parallel the political line, with children and women grouped among the powerless who, especially those of the lower classes, remain victims of the powerful. The environment is also at risk with the Chernobyl disaster in *The Cloning of Joanna May* and the pig farms and faulty nuclear plant in rural England in *The Heart of the Country*. Technology, war, and economics begin to figure in her view of postmodern society as she portrays a world controlled by corrupt politicians, technocrats, and media lords.

The Shrapnel Academy

Weldon has described *The Shrapnel Academy* as "a fairly overt political act. . . . Of all the novels, it is the one where I set out to do something political" (Kumar, 16). The allegorical novel satirizes the history of warfare and weaponry, set in "an institution dedicated to the memory of that great military genius Henry Shrapnel—he who in 1804 invented the exploding cannonball" (7). It is a veritable catalog of military strategy, including background on the so-called great men who have created diverse and terrible ways of winning wars, including Napoleon, Alexander, and Shrapnel himself. The cataloguing, tedious in its loyalty to detail and accuracy, is related by a first-person narrator who integrates her history lesson into a rather fantastical story of a group who come to the academy for a lecture by a General Leo Makeshift on the "Decisive Battles of World War II" (7). Joan Lumb, the custodian, has invited the unlikely group to a dinner at the academy on the night before the lecture.

The academy houses an uncertain number of immigrants who work and live below the first floor. They represent the underprivileged classes, mostly of darker skin, who have found refuge there. Many are illegal immigrants, brought there to safety by the legal ones, and are unbeknownst to Joan, who thinks her staff consists of 36 servants and employees. "The Shrapnel servants slept in dormitories in the semi-basement and basement which made up the kitchen and service areas of the great house. And if they slept five to a bed, and six under it, Joan Lumb was not to know. Their children were trained not to cough or cry when she was on her monthly round of dormitory inspection. Old ladies stayed their wheezing and old men their coughing, while Joan Lumb strode by. They pressed themselves into the cupboards and alcoves of this dank, subterranean world, and lived to see another day" (45–46). The symbolic setting contrasts this group with the guests upstairs, the privileged, who are to be served by those of the lower class. Acorn, the butler from Soweto, is the leader and representative of the oppressed ones, declaring war in the kitchen below while the statused guests drink and eat on the floor above. Postulating the abuses of his oppressors, he rounds off his speech to the staff by declaring, "We will eat the dinner party!" (131). Acorn though is forestalled by a staff member, Inverness, who objects to his vitriol and rhetoric of war. Inverness and his cohorts assail Acorn, dosing him with psychotic drugs in order to bring an end to his incipient revolution.

Despite its sardonic tone and serious subject matter, the novel, with its ridiculous situations that unsettle us on one level and make us laugh on another, is humorous. When the servants feed the guests a dog pâté made from one of the guest's pets, Harry, the situation is amusing because much has been made of the European view of the subterranean nature of other cultures. One guest remarks that they eat dogs "there," while the group itself devours caribou, turkey and salmon without conscience. The novel also points out that Harry, in the hierarchy of the academy's occupants, falls at the bottom, ignored by his owners and victim of those who fathom themselves at a higher scale in the schema of living beings.

The novel successfully conveys the insanity of warfare and the unreserved prejudice of the privileged, white classes, but it is less satisfying in its resolution of the conflict between the groups. When the above-ground group imagine themselves under attack by the servants, they defend themselves, creating a war council and blowing up the entire academy, including everyone except two—a chauffeur and a feminist journalist. Although the novel has set up its own ending by establishing the irrational and absurd conflict between the groups, that very predictability oversimplifies the narrative resolution. Certainly Weldon has tried to establish some middle ground where the two have not established alliances with either group yet represent the oppressed (servant and woman); nonetheless, we are left with a feeling of indifference for these two who remain. Why should the feminist and the chauffeur survive a holocaust when we know that in the real world catastrophes are arbitrary in the selection of survivors?

The Cloning of Joanna May

The Cloning of Joanna May depicts a postmodern world with scientific and technological advancements that have brought humankind to the verge of ecological holocaust. The novel's horror arises from the misuse of these advancements by powerful men, especially Carl May, a sinister technocrat whose company rehabilitates nuclear power stations. Carl's money and prestige have allowed him to take advantage of the current scientific discoveries, using them for solipsistic motives. In the beginning of the novel, the Chernobyl meltdown has just occurred, and May, as the spokesman for his company, uses the media to placate the fears of the public, downplaying the dangers of the accident. In these press releases he lies unreservedly: " 'It can't happen here. Our reactors are constructed on a different principle from theirs. Children may safely drink milk though sheep may no longer safely graze on the uplands.' His lies were soft and persuasive, as ever: and his face calm and handsome" (47). Carl's rhetoric satirizes corporate representatives who equivocate, using the media to deceive the public regarding ecological damage caused by industrial accidents.

Carl's evil, godlike impulses are most apparent when he has his former wife, Joanna May, cloned. During an ersatz abortion for a false pregnancy, he has a Dr. Holly clone her, producing four eggs, which are then placed in different women. The children grow up in varied circumstances, unaware of their origins. Carl's cruelty toward others is explained by his childhood upbringing; he was raised in a kennel, was suckled on a dog for sustenance, and found kinship with the other pups. Carl's cruel, absurd upbringing shows the effects of parenting on adult behavior. When married to Joanna, he kills her dogs out of jealousy and later has his chauffeur run over her lover, Isaac, killing him. Carl has no remorse for these pathological acts, and his insanity grows as the novel progresses. Carl exemplifies the evil present in postmodern society. Joanna defines evil as "the absence of God" (46). God, she explains, has flown off, despairing of humankind, leaving the evil ones like Carl to impersonate God. Carl's malevolence, his absolute lack of compassion, is a result of his abused childhood. A culture that does not love its children perpetuates those, like Carl, who use power as a substitute for love.

Joanna May does not learn of the clones until after her divorce, during a brutal fight with Carl. When she brags to him about her new lover, he tells her of the clones, then, like a vampire, attacks her: "[H]e dug his yellow fangs into Joanna's neck just above her genteel string of pearls and he scraped up a piece of her skin with those disgusting teeth and went to the little designer fridge where he kept his whisky (for guests) and his Perrier (for him) and he took out a little box and with a spatula scraped the flesh, the living tissue, of Joanna May off the teeth and shook it into the box with a short sharp shake and put it back in the fridge and said now I'll grow you into what I want, he said, I can and will, see how you like that, I'll make you live in pain and shame for ever more, I have brought hell to earth" (110). Arriving home, Joanna finds her lover, Oliver, dead, strung up by his feet in the barn. At 60, Joanna determines to find the clones, now 30, and begins her search for Dr. Holly, who holds the secrets to her multiple selves.

Joanna articulates Weldon's critique of postmodern culture, her analysis becoming more acute and introspective after she learns of the clones. This splitting of her identity, which she refers to as the "I," unsettles her view of selfhood and she sees in contemporary society a similar displacement. TV, for example, has fractured the "I" of identity, producing images that encourage conformity, or scenes of violence that kill individuality. All that is left is an audience, a perverse collective, ingesting the falsehoods of the glowing TV screen: "Our little shard, our little divine shred of identity, so precariously held, is altogether lost as we join the oneness that is audience. My clones and I. After I found out about the clones I began to worry a lot about 'I' " (46). Joanna expresses the importance of seeing on the human personality in a pun on the human eye. She tells the story of a girl who, in prison "doing three years for cheque offences, plucked out her eye" (20). It is what the girl has viewed in prison that has brought her to this act: "three years of looking at old Tampaxes in corners and cigarette stubs and grime and grey tins holding the brown slime of institution stew" (21). Similarly, the eye of contemporary society, inundated by advertising and pop-culture iconography such as Mickey Mouse, forms the "I" of the self through vision. What contemporary society sees, then, leads to a psychic destruction: "If the I offend thee pluck it out. Idopectomy" (46).

Joanna's commentary depicts postmodern society as enamored by reproductions, replicas that bury the individual beneath layers of images and ersatz messages. Cloning is one of science's contributions to this hyperreal world that steals away human uniqueness. Being born no longer carries with it the genetic nuances of parenting and womb. In this futuristic world, individuality is shared by numerous others whose DNA is an exact copy of the original. Control and power are the objectives of those who try to create a world of sameness: identical beliefs and behavior sell commodities fueling the marketplace. Corporations feast on feeble minds that digest the carefully crafted ideology of progress and production. By cloning Joanna May, Carl has attempted to control her love for him: "They'd love him as Joanna had. Of course they would: they were Joanna. When he multiplied her he had not so much tried to multiply perfection—that was a tale for Holly—he had done it to multiply her love for him, Joanna May's love for Carl May, multiply it fourfold: to make up for what he'd never had: Carl May, the bitch's son" (241).

Carl's effort to reproduce Joanna for his own selfish purposes, ironically, has the opposite effect of his intentions. Rather than diminishing her worth, the clones enhance her life and are responsible for his demise. When Joanna discovers their existence she experiences an epiphany: "When I acknowledged my sisters, my twins, my clones, my children, when I stood out against Carl May, I found myself: pop! I was out. He thought he would diminish me: he couldn't: he made me" (246). Trying to kill Joanna's selfhood by creating those identical to her, Carl actually helps his former wife to discover herself. Symbolically, the clones are the repressed aspects of Joanna that she has not realized. The surfacing of her multifarious selves gives her vision, and she understands that Carl must be stopped. Hearing of Carl's plan to jump into a cooling pool at one of his nuclear plants as a media hype to prove the harmlessness of radiation, she contacts one of his cohorts, arranging to have some fuel rods not quite spent of their energy placed in the pool. Radiated, Carl indeed dies, but not before he asks Joanna to have him cloned. With Dr. Holly's help, she fulfills his request and the result is young Carl, whom Joanna raises as her own.

Joanna's fragmented self, evident in the clones, Alice, Julie, Gina, and Jane, additionally refers to the potential kinship among women. Upon meeting, Joanna and the clones identify with one another in mutual suffering and experience. As Joanna explains, "We are one woman split five ways, a hundred ways, a million million ways" (265). The discovery of one another symbolically engages Joanna and the clones in finding themselves in other women, and in so doing, they find comfort and support: "They could see now that was the trouble—they'd been lonely. They used men to stop them being lonely. No wonder it all went wrong. Now they had each other, nothing need be the same" (251). The clones form a community, helping one another with child rearing and offering respite from bad relationships. Joanna has the help of Alice, for example, who gives birth to Carl's clone.

Joanna, then, escapes Carl's evil plan to take away her individuality. More victoriously, when Joanna clones Carl she rewrites the past, giving her former husband the chance to grow up in a loving environment. Her reproduction though, unlike Carl's, is not for selfish ends but to enact a kind of salvation to remedy the ills of the past. She understands that children have potential beyond their genetic imprint: they are innocent creatures vulnerable to teaching. She recognizes the capacity for evil in all human beings, including herself, but attempts to transcend that impulse. Observing little Carl, she wants to punish him for wrongs done by her former husband: "I could beat him black and blue, and am still sometimes tempted to, to punish him for what he did to me, for the unlived life he gave me, so many years of it, the guilt he made me feel, the loss he made me endure, for the deaths of Isaac and of Oliver. Except this innocent has done nothing: I know he could, that's all, and knowing what he could do also know what I could do, sufficiently provoked; and so I have to forgive him, both in retrospect and in advance" (263). And so Joanna addresses a central quandary of human existence. The potential for evil resides within all of us and is especially seductive when we respond to past wrongs by hurting others. There must be a corrective, and the only way to transcend vengeance is to forgive, to love when the desire to salve pain invites retribution.

Darcy's Utopia

Darcy's Utopia juxtaposes the economic-social theories of the heroine, Eleanor Darcy, with the love story of two journalists who are both interviewing her for their respective magazines. Hugo Vanistart, a political journalist, is seeking a story grounded in economic theory, Darcian Monetarism, for his intellectual audience. Valerie Jones, a features editor for a leading women's magazine, focuses on the woman's angle and is also writing a biography of Eleanor. The two journalists meet at an awards banquet, fall in love, and move into a Holiday Inn together, where they stay while interviewing the famous Eleanor. The novel's structure shifts from question-answer interviews, to Valerie's first-person commentary, to the biography she's writing about the famous woman, entitled *Lovers at the Gate*.

As the biography develops we learn that Eleanor was born Apricot Smith on a backstreet of London. When her mother, Wendy, leaves her father, Ken, a banjo player, for another man, Eleanor's grandmother Rhoda moves in with Ken, thus "Apricot's mother became her sister, and her grandmother her mother" (41). Her name becomes Ellen Parkin when she marries a fervent, proselytizing Catholic boy named Bernard Parkin, to whom she is married for 17 years. A few years later he converts to Marxism, showing the same spirited involvement that he had once applied to his religion.

Eleanor's fame derives from her second husband, Julian Darcy, an economist and former vice chancellor at the University of Bridport, who changes her name to Eleanor. An adviser to the prime minister, he has enacted an economic policy that has threatened the financial stability of the nation. We assume at the novel's outset that Eleanor is the spokesperson for her husband's theories, but as the interviews and biography develop, we realize that her utopian vision is personal, born of years of hardship and political study while married to her first husband, Bernard. It would seem that the men in Eleanor's life are the thinkers, but subversively she is the analyst whose worldview transcends theirs. In fact, Bernard eschews Catholicism and later Marxism because of his wife's rabid adherence and purist dedication to the tenets of each. When he wants to take a vacation, she accuses him of being bourgeois, reminding him of the working masses who would attend them in their pursuit of pleasure. Worn down, he finally relents to become a capitalist.

Hugo and Valerie are enamored by Eleanor, and the journalists' love affair is fueled by their association with her. Abandoning wife, husband, and children, Valerie and Hugo forswear their ordinary lives to hole up in the hotel, caught up in the mystical narrative that allows them an escape from their mediocre lives and fuels their sexual attraction for each other. They experience a love described by Eleanor in her first interview with Hugo: "[L]ove is enough to make you believe in God. It is the evidence you need which proves the benign nature of the universe. Love heightens your perceptions: it makes the air you breathe beautiful. It lets you know you are alive" (7). Of course Eleanor is describing the early stages of falling in love, a temporary state that the two lovers believe is eternal. As Eleanor relates her own love stories, the ephemeral nature of this feeling is revealed. Illusions, though, are seductive and Eleanor knows how to weave them. Truth may reside in Eleanor's philosophy, but as her friend Brenda says, "[I]t's sometimes hard to tell when she's joking and when she isn't" (188).

It is in the ambiguity of Eleanor's theories that we find Weldon's social analysis. Easily, one could say that we don't know when Weldon is joking. Her heroine's utopia is both wise and ridiculous, explained in part by Eleanor's defense that "[s]ometimes I get things wrong. How can I not? I'm human" (226). Here, Eleanor admits what few profit-philosophers will: that truth is negotiable. Further, this admission contradicts the very idea of utopia—that a perfect world can in fact exist. Darcy's utopia is an amalgam of theories drawn from a variety of belief systems. This quality is its imaginative base and its unsettling source of confusion. It does not wholly agree with any one ideology. Eleanor's disparate views arise, too, in the joint interviews. Her ideas, though not haphazard, come in pieces, lacking the coherence of a whole system. She believes that the primary and most tenable cause of social ills is money, which is "the source of all pain" (36). Unpredictably, it is not the lack of money that Eleanor finds harmful but the presence of money as a motivating force. She does not take a liberal stance, which would ask that money be taken from the rich and given to the poor or that the downtrodden deserve better recompense for work. Instead, in her utopia "there will be no wages, there will be no money" (37). Devaluing money, she posits, will obliterate class differences rather than heighten them: "[M]erely increase the supply of money until it becomes something of little value, as plentiful as grass: let it grow on every street corner, pour from the high street banks: see how little by little it is of less and less value" (37). Eleanor attacks the two most powerful economic theories of our century: capitalism and Marxism. Money itself, the empty symbol, must be proliferated until it has no meaning, no significance.

That idea underlies Darcian Monetarism, and when Julian Darcy puts this theory to practice to remedy a depressed economy, he causes the collapse of the government and ends up in jail. After persuading the government that his approach is valid, the government, on a Sunday, disseminates notes from bank cash dispensers across the nation. Those who need the money take it and pay their bills, and the dissatisfied workers do not go to their jobs on Monday. Alarmed, the bureaucrats stop issuing the money, which according to Julian is why his approach did not work. The effect of the aborted plan is chaos: "The Prime Minister resigned: the EEC put in a stop-gap government of bureaucrats: martial law was briefly imposed: a new currency introduced" (217). In this ridiculous scenario, Weldon satirizes governmental regulatory policies that are meant to stimulate the economy. As Julian explains, " 'We devalue the pound but only on paper. We use it to make people poor, not rich.' " (214). Devaluing the pound may give people more money, but it is of less value, a consequence that affects the poor, with the rich being unaffected because their supply of money is unthreatened. Eleanor explains to Julian that " '[t]o make the poor rich is to make the rich poor' " (214). From this statement Julian realizes that to make money cheap and accessible to all, the government must give it away.

The concept of Eleanor's utopian society that bothers her interviewers the most is her view of childbearing. In her utopia all babies will be aborted unless the community decides that the parents will be adequate. As Eleanor tells Hugo, "The decision to 'choose,' or not to 'choose' will be taken away from parents and left to an ad-hoc committee of neighbours" (133). Here we see Weldon upsetting feminist and fundamentalist views of abortion rights while in a sense merging them. Eleanor does not abjure abortion as wholly wrong nor does she believe it is the mother's right to decide. She takes a middle ground that evokes an authority, the community, to decide what is best for the child—abortion is sanctioned by those other than the parents. Weldon takes moral imperatives from both groups and merges them into one rather absurd tenet, creating a kind of hybrid ethics leveled at both camps. Weldon implies that these are difficult issues, not easily resolved through dogma or self-righteous pronouncements. Weldon has described Eleanor Darcy as "all feminist thought taken to its extreme. She is in the business of starting a religion. And using a man to do it. I can see she's not much of a feminist. She's a realist, or a pragmatist. Anyway, she's not really male or female; she's androgynous, as far as I'm concerned. She's a wicked fascist" (Kumar, 16).

We must doubt the salience of Eleanor's utopia because its dogma does not address the problems of those who live in the real world. In contrast, the unpretentious, peripheral character Brenda has a more benevolent, less didactic social vision. Brenda has children and little time to live in the quixotic world of philosophy, referring to Darcy's utopia as a "crazy vision" offering a brief synopsis of her own utopia: "I want a world fit for my kids to grow up in. Look, I want a world for *me* to grow up in. . . . I want to believe that my daily life has a purpose which is more than just me" (188–89). Brenda admires Eleanor for her perceptions but also recognizes her friend's lack of being in touch with the real lives of those she would seem to care about.

When Valerie finishes *Lover at the Gate,* her love affair with Hugo comes " to a full stop" (222), and when the two meet in the hotel lobby, they barely recognize each other. Finishing her book, Valerie is released from Eleanor's spell, which has been responsible for her affair with Hugo. Valerie returns to her family but later discovers that Hugo has founded a new Darcinian religion. Attending one of his sermons, she finds that Hugo has turned Eleanor's ideas into "commandments" (234). Like the other men in Eleanor's life, Hugo seeks certainties, trying to establish truth in ideologies. Eleanor's slippery doctrines elude them all, however, a mottled canvas entrapping the truth seeker in its whimsical labyrinth. Valerie, though, has escaped the seductive call of Eleanor Darcy's religion, recognizing, like Brenda, "How could you ever tell when Eleanor Darcy was joking, or when she was serious?" (234).

Darcy's Utopia depicts the 1990s as a time of conflicting theories, failed ethics, and a paucity of visionaries to offer hope. Eleanor Darcy imagines a utopia that reveals the shortcomings of a culture of haves and have-nots, where people impose their own ethics on one another, proclaiming the rightness, the godliness of their views. Perhaps the latter is the central target of the novel's satire, when ideology becomes the equivalent of a religion. Valerie, with the clarity of skepticism, walks away from Hugo, past a woman in a car outside the house where he is preaching. Though she believes the woman may be Eleanor, she walks on, realizing: "I could not ever come to worship and adore Eleanor Darcy as Hugo did, but I could sure as hell admire her spirit" (235).

The Heart of the Country

The Heart of the Country is narrated by Sonia, who has been placed in a mental institution after setting a float on fire in a Guy Fawkes carnival parade, killing the carnival princess. An irreverent, sardonic speaker and a churlish social critic, Sonia tells the story of Natalie, an upper-class woman whose husband fails to return home after work, having run off with a local carnival queen, leaving his wife with unpaid bills, a house with outstanding tax debts, and a car with payments in arrears. Natalie, left homeless, carless, and penniless with two children to care for, must apply for social welfare to support her family. Sonia, having been abandoned by her husband after her own infidelity, lives on welfare and tutors Natalie on how to survive on state support. *The Heart of the Country* is pointedly political, quoting statistics about the financial inequities of divorced women: "About 40 percent of men are strangely enough better off after a divorce than before, while 80 percent of divorced women with dependent children are 60 percent worse off" (32). Indeed, Natalie, one of the worse off, her house sold for unpaid taxes and her car repossessed, is left with nothing to do but turn to the state to support her. Bureaucratic stumbling blocks lead her to move in with Sonia, sending her children to public schools and giving the family dog away because she cannot afford to feed him. Paralleling the lives of Natalie and Sonia are Angus, an estate agent, and Arthur, an antique dealer, who control property in the town, acquiring their power by "[b]uying and selling, property and land, jobs for the boys on the Town Council, drinking with the planners in the pub—nothing went on that Arthur and Angus didn't know about, nothing happened they didn't want to see happen" (33). When Natalie loses her home, it is Arthur and Angus who take advantage: Arthur buys her house at a good price, reselling it later for a profit, and Angus auctions the house's furnishings at bargain prices for his friends and colleagues.

The theme of female guilt runs through *The Heart of the Country,* with the women accepting responsibility for being abandoned by men, and the social institutions affirming that fact. The women must have done something wrong, the bureaucrat implies, or they would not be in need of state support. Bureaucrats punish and threaten women by doling out money arbitrarily and demanding submission from those in need. The first line of the novel, "Oh, the wages of sin!," reflects the attitude of self-punishing women reckoning themselves rampant sinners: "The first thing a woman who suffers misfortune feels is *guilty*. My *fault*, she is convinced. *Something I did wrong*" (13). Natalie blames herself when her husband leaves, as do others in the community, assuming she is being punished for having an affair with Arthur. In contrast, men, according to Sonia, take no responsibility: "Ever heard a man say, 'It was my fault the marriage broke up'? No. Those are women's lines. They'll stare at you with their black eyes and broken noses and say, 'My fault! I provoked him' " (77). Unfaithful wives suffer retributions for their infidelities. Their husband's betrayals, however, must be tolerated by wives who depend on them for economic well-being.

Similarly, Sonia claims that the poor and downtrodden are blamed for their powerlessness and dependence, ill-treated for their failure to rise in the class system. As Natalie's son, Ben, has learned from his father's view of the lower classes, " 'Why do people like that always live in such a mess? . . . It doesn't cost anything just to tidy it up, does it? But they'd rather live off the rest of us than lift a finger for themselves' " (29). The novel persists in describing the sadomasochistic urge that exists in the division of power. The moneyed can justify the poor wages they pay to menial workers by labeling them incompetent; the caretakers of mental patients can justify their cruel treatment of their wards because they have apparently done something wrong; and the oppressed collude in their own mistreatment by feeling guilty about their lowly status. The symbiotic pattern persists with little class transgression, especially in the case of men and women whose relationships reflect economic and sexual expediency. Women are sexual and domestic servants in return for economic solvency. Natalie, for example, eventually growing weary of her desperate, impoverished lifestyle, agrees to become Angus's mistress, and he provides her with a fine apartment in return for sexual favors.

Sonia's ironic commentary undercuts the self-effacing attitude of women and the self-aggrandizing behavior of men. Skillfully she survives in the system but continues to resist the subservience expected of her. Her eventual rebellion results in actual imprisonment in a mental institution after she rallies a group of women to resist their oppressors. Having been hired by Angus and Arthur to build a float with a symbolic virgin, Mrs. Housewife Princess, she tells the women that they should "stop colluding" with men in their oppression. Weldon evokes a carnival atmosphere (alluding to Guy Fawkes) to incite the women to action: "Of their own accord, out of their own oppression, they were back in the ancient spirit of carnival, when the images of the hated were paraded through the streets, and hung from gibbets, or rolled down the hills in burning tar barrels" (189). It is Sonia's idea to make effigies of the images of Angus and Arthur, portraying them as ridiculous figures. Yelling to the crowd, she tells them "[t]hat they lived here in the heart of the country in the shadow of cruise missiles, in the breeze from Hinkley Point. That it was up to the women to fight back, because the men had lost their nerve" (194). The crowd cheers, recognizing the absurd symbolism of the parasitical property owners who take advantage of the less fortunate. When Sonia sets Angus's effigy on fire, she fulfills the purpose of carnival but unwittingly causes the death of Flora, the housekeeping princess. Sonia has not intended anyone to be hurt, but she recognizes that in effect Flora's death is symbolically a "virgin sacrifice" (196). Weldon overturns the patriarchal virgin sacrifice, giving the rite to women who burn the concomitant image of housewife and virgin, reclaiming their own self-definition. Ann Hebert offers a fine reading of Weldon's use of carnival in the novel: "Historically, carnival was contained within the established order—an outlet which was sanctioned, even demanded by the authorities, a transgression generated and even required by the law. However, Weldon's carnivalesque text refuses to be contained and leaves the reader with a lingering sense of dis-ease. Carnival for Weldon is not merely a reversal of hierarchies that will revert again to the 'natural' order of masculine supremacy once the laughter dies down. Weldon critiques the very assumptions of hierarchy—a critique that remains unresolved at the end of her texts" (Hebert, 27).

Having destroyed the iconography of male privilege, Sonia is committed to a mental institution. In yet another happy ending, Weldon sets her subversive antagonist free when her psychiatrist proposes marriage and declares her sane. But "[s]he can't accept of course. Happy endings are not so easy. No she must get on with changing the world, rescuing the country. There is no time left for frivolity" (201). Sonia the outcast, the madwoman, prevails, having recognized the corrupt power system that has kept women economically powerless, relegating them to housewife and whore. All may not be well in the heart of the country, but at least one woman recognizes the wrongdoing and chooses to act, to speak out against social inequities, to urge resistance to self-blame among the powerless.

Chapter Seven

Creating the Story:
Happy Coincidences

Doesn't simply nothing happen for ages—and then everything happen
all at once, excitingly or terribly, as the case may be?
(*The Hearts and Lives of Men*, 188)

In the following four works of the late '80s and early '90s, Weldon
experiments with self-conscious narrative structures that put fiction
writing at the forefront of their concerns. I include in this group *Letters
to Alice*—a nonfiction work—for its concern with literary aesthetics. The
book comprises letters written by the narrator, Aunt Fay, to her niece
Alice, who has recently encountered Jane Austen in a college English literature course. Aunt Fay, a novelist, provides a straightforward view of
the role of the fiction writer. Though numerous novels allude to the relationship between art and life, *Letters to Alice* reveals Weldon's aesthetics.
Nor does the author aim for ambiguity on this point, having named the
narrator after herself and including autobiographical references. Yet as
always we must read Weldon with an ear to irony. She explains to her
niece, for example, that readers want "moral guidance" not coincidence,
because "[c]oincidence happens in real life all the time. Not here. Cause
and effect must rule, or else the readers will prefer reality, with its chaos
and coincidence" (68). Most of Weldon's novels, though, commingle
both. Coincidences occur as in real life, but Weldon often manipulates
the plot to create happy endings for her female characters. It is the
attention to this discrepancy between life and art that Weldon plays on,
suggesting that the happy ending may satisfy us, but it has nothing in
common with real life.

Similar techniques are found in the construction of *The Hearts and
Lives of Men*, *Life Force*, and *Growing Rich*, novels that give us narrators
who ponder the relationship between life and art. In *The Heart and Lives
of Men*, an unnamed narrator repeatedly interrupts her story to give
advice and talk about the ongoing events. Promising a happy ending,

she creates a plot based on coincidence, advising that such incidents are not unlike life: "Reader, you know how in real life coincidence happens again and again. Your sister and your son's wife have the same birthday; on the day you meet a long-lost friend, by accident in the street, a letter from that same friend arrives; your boss's wife was born in the house you now live in—that kind of thing! It's against commonly accepted rules for writers to use coincidence in fiction, but I hope you will bear with me..." (188).

In *Life Force* Nora interrupts the third-person narration to tell the reader that she is writing a book; she shifts in and out of her narrative with commentary, admitting that she is imagining the thoughts and feelings of the characters. Similarly, in *Growing Rich* the wheelchair-bound Hattie, with no active life of her own, imagines events in the lives of the characters she observes through her window: "Sometimes I wonder whether in fact it's I myself, sitting in my window, who control their lives, and not just fate" (7). To some degree, all of Weldon's fiction points to the artifice of narrative, but in this group of novels, the narrators bring the creation of their stories to the reader's attention. In both *The Hearts and Lives of Men* and *Life Force,* artists and art play a significant part in the novels' thematic concerns, mocking the art world populated by the vain and insipid, who have little truck with aesthetics. *The Hearts and Lives of Men* takes place within the marketplace of art, with two narcissistic figures, an art dealer and an angry artist who vie for power; and *Life Force* revolves around a painting that brings a former group of friends together again. The value of art objects and the concept of good and bad art complement the novels' concerns with writing as artifice.

Letters to Alice: On First Reading Jane Austen

Alice, 18, has in a previous letter described Austen as "boring, petty and irrelevant" (7). Aunt Fay's letters to her niece defend Austen's novels with detailed descriptions of the society of eighteenth- and nineteenth-century England and vivid accounts of the author's life. Autobiographical references occur in the novel. In one example Aunt Fay refers to her reading audiences: "How, audiences say to me, can you be married and have sons and still be so horrible about men? And I reply, (a) 'I am not horrible to and about men, I merely report them as I see them. I neither condone nor reproach, I merely report. It's just that men are so accustomed to being flattered in books by women that simple honesty comes as a shock and they register it as biased and unfair'—and if they don't let me get away with that I retreat to, (b) 'This is a literary truth, not a home truth. The writer is not the person, yet both natures are true' " (97). This question is one Weldon is frequently asked. Part b of her answer is echoed in interviews in which she reiterates that the persona of any book is to be distinguished from the author herself.

Letters to Alice is an entertaining, interesting read, with vivid historical descriptions of Jane Austen's England, focusing on the condition of women at the time. The aunt is attempting to give her niece a background from which to read the author, yet the scholarly information is balanced with a lively tone that renders social history fascinating and sometimes shocking. Contrasting Alice's contemporary life with Jane's, she explains that for a woman "to marry was a great prize. It was a woman's aim. . . . Once you were married of course, life was not rosy. Any property you did acquire belonged to your husband. The children were his, not yours. If the choice at childbirth was between the mother or child, the mother was the one to go" (27–28). Aunt Fay further tries to defend Austen's preoccupation with polite society in her fiction, pointing out that Austen incorporated subtle truths into her novel that defied the conventions of the time: "She believed it was better not to marry at all, than to marry without love. Such notions were quite new at the time" (25).

The most evocative element of the book is Aunt Fay's attempt to define "Literature," using the metaphorical "City of Invention" to describe the body of works of the great writers where "writers create Houses of the Imagination, from whose doors the generations greet each other" (12), advising that to understand Austen "you do need to be, just a little, acquainted with the City: at any rate with its more important districts" (15). Delicately, Aunt Fay informs her niece of a literary tradition, suggesting that her engagement with reading must go beyond her own limited interests. One does not read well without contextualizing, and without the understanding that the great works of literature speak to one another through similar concerns. As an aunt and not a parent, Fay wants to avoid pronouncements, aware that the young find their own generational preoccupations more seductive than the backdrop of history. The letters read like a lively lecture commingled with the personal connections the women share.

Above all, fiction should enlighten readers, thus improving society in general. It should, for example, promote empathy, especially in the upper classes: "The gentry, then as now, *has* to read in order to comprehend both the wretchedness and the ire of the multitude. It is not only ignorance in the illiterate we need to combat, it is insensitivity in the well-to-do" (77). In responding to her niece's question of what makes a good novel, Fay evokes the term "moral guidance," explaining that readers want fiction to help them understand themselves, yet want the good to prevail, while the bad suffer. She admits this is not the way life is but that readers try to escape the coincidences of reality by reading fiction seeking actions and events that are meaningful. We find this same tenet in Weldon's works in which heroines or antiheroines have, if not gloriously happy outcomes, at least liberating experiences, escaping bad marriages and dangerous situations when they act benevolently or come to personal awareness.

In a final irony Alice writes a popular novel, one more successful than Fay's books; Fay tells her: "You have sold more copies of *The Wife's Revenge* in three months than I have all of my novels put together" (125). The success of her niece's book highlights an underlying suggestion in Fay's letters. Readers of popular fiction (generally unacquainted with the City of Invention) do not buy books to be enlightened, but want what Fay told her niece not to write about—the love story between Alice and her professor. The public wants romance, a distasteful truth that Weldon repeatedly disavows with the greatest force in *The Life and Loves of a She-Devil*.

The Hearts and Lives of Men

The Hearts and Lives of Men begins "Reader, I am going to tell you the story of Clifford, Helen and little Nell" (1). The first-person narrator is the self-admitted creator of the story, distanced from the events, commenting on the characters' actions, drawing attention to the narrative's fictional structure. This unnamed narrator's tone is more conversational than ironic, her intrusive commentary largely about how stories are constructed and the readers' expectations. She prepares us in the beginning for a happy ending: "There! You know already this story is to have a happy ending. But it's Christmastime. Why not?" (1). To Weldon's credit, revealing the ending does not diminish the plot's seductive hold on the reader. She effectively creates sympathy for the child Nell, who must experience many fateful events before she finds the happiness promised by the narrator. In fact, it is our desire to see Nell triumph over evil forces that carries the narrative line and, as Weldon has predicted, demonstrates our desire for happy endings. Goodness will prevail in Nell's world: "Evil circles good, as if trying to contain it: good being the powerful, moving, active force, and evil the nagging, restraining one. Well, you must make up your own mind as you read Nell's story. This is a Christmas tale, and Christmas is a time for believing in good, rather than bad: for seeing the former, not the latter, on the winning side" (40). Life does not operate like fiction, but the author through plot contrivances can create fortuitous circumstances. Further, Weldon suggests—even while giving her characters a happy ending— that human beings create their own circumstances. Life is not art, but art can show us how to behave in a way that avoids at least some degree of suffering for ourselves and others. Once again, Weldon uses children to show the effect of our actions on others: the innocent are vulnerable and deserve our most rapt attention to their lives.

Nell is the daughter of Clifford and Helen, who experience love at first sight, conceive Nell, marry, and soon divorce because of infidelities and misjudgments. Nell's parents' stormy relationship puts Nell's life in peril, and she becomes a pawn in their competitive love-hate relationship. Losing legal custody of his daughter, Clifford hires a man named Blount to kidnap her and take her to Clifford's home in Switzerland. On the way there Blount and Nell survive a plane crash, though they are presumed dead. After Blount sells four-year-old Nell for illegal adoption, she lives in a series of homes and is nurtured by a rather eccentric group of people, narrowly escaping harm as she moves from place to place. While she is gone her parents' tumultuous relationship continues over the years, as they still love one another, and they remarry at one point only to divorce again.

Nell's perilous journey through life until she is reunited with her parents at age 18 reminds us of Liffey's baby in *Puffball*, who survives the assaults of Mab and the various physical changes of the womb that threaten her existence. *The Hearts and Lives of Men* puts a multifarious host of dangers in Nell's path, which she narrowly escapes, her survival a result of favorable coincidences. Before being aborted by her mother, Clifford arrives, heroically carrying Helen out of the clinic before she undergoes the procedure. When the plane crashes, Nell and her kidnapper remain belted to their seats in the tail of the plane, which lands on the ocean in shallow water. Nell also survives a house fire, a car wreck, and the attack of vicious dogs, examples of exceptional rescues that may be the stuff of adventure but not human existence. It is this exaggeration, the self-conscious manipulation of the story to bring about Nell's salvation, that reminds us of how perilous the world is for children. In this way the novel resembles a moral tale, advice to parents about child rearing, such as when the narrator addresses the reader on the issue of punishing children: "I never knew anyone, child or adult, who was 'punished' and was better for the experience. Punishment is inflicted by the powerful upon the powerless. It breeds defiance, sulking, fear and hatred, but never remorse, reform or self-understanding. It makes matters worse, not better. It adds to the sum total of human misery; it cannot possibly subtract from it" (250). In passages like this one, the narrator offers straightforward advice with no hint of irony, for children are indeed a serious matter.

On the other hand, the narrator refers to the accidents of life that outdo fiction in their unlikelihood: "This story of mine follows real life pretty closely—which is why it may at times seem farfetched. Ask yourself, isn't truth even more unbelieveable than fiction? Don't the headlines which greet you every day, in your daily newspaper, speak of the most extraordinary and unlikely events? Don't events cluster in your life? Doesn't simply nothing happen for ages—and then everything happen all at once, excitingly or terribly, as the case may be? Well, it certainly does in mine, and writers can be no different from readers" (188). These playful references once again remind us that fiction is merely a representation of life. This idea agrees with Weldon's narrative experiments that continue to use form to undermine our association with fiction and life, showing how works of literature can enlighten us.

Weldon's concern with the aesthetics of literature is also reflected in her presentation of artists and the art world. *The Hearts and Lives of Men* takes place within the marketplace of art, with Clifford as the quintessential art dealer who manipulates the value of art for his own self-interest. Helen's father, John Lally, represents the surly, angry artist who produces his eccentric, violent art outside the powerful art enclave of Leonardo's marshaled by Clifford. The artistic narcissism of the two lampoons both dealer and artist, as they vie for power, with the actual creative act lost in the struggle between two self-centered men. To Clifford, art is for profit, and though perspicacious in his ability to identify a van Gogh retrieved from an attic, he fails to appreciate the beauty and the joy of artistic production. Lally, the eccentric artist, is no more admirable, persecuting his daughter and wife through bouts of creative genius. He locks himself in his garage, refusing to talk to anyone, while his compliant wife brings him food, defending his behavior because he is an artist. In contrast to other Weldon male characters, however, both Clifford and Lally experience some degree of transformation during the course of the novel and change their selfish ways. Clifford by the end of the novel begins to express love and compassion for Helen and his children, and John's behavior is tempered by a second wife. These transformations in character are, to a degree, inevitable because the book has promised the reader a happy ending.

Life Force

Life Force is narrated by Nora, a clerical worker, who is composing a novel of the same title while doing part-time clerical work for a realty company. The book describes a network of friends who have known each other for close to 20 years, having lived in the same neighborhood in the '70s. The focus of the story and the symbolic figure to which the title refers is Leslie Beck, a charismatic, sexually rapacious man, a satyr, who has affairs with most of the women of the group, including Nora, and has fathered a child with almost all of them. On the surface, "life force" refers to Leslie's abundant procreative and magnetic energy that makes him irresistible to women. Although sexuality is the central subject of the novel, with numerous descriptions, for example, of Leslie's penis and the sexual escapades of the characters, "life force" refers to deeper human longings, to the energy that motivates human desire. Nora explains Leslie's life force in this way: "Leslie Beck's Life Force is the energy not so much of sexual desire as of sexual discontent: the urge to find someone better out there, and thereby something better in the self, the one energy working against the other, creating a find and animating friction" (13).

Through her accounts of Leslie's sexual prowess, we learn more about Nora than we do the other characters. She admits that she is attempting to write an autobiographical–biographical story focusing on first-person accounts from the point of view of Marion Loos, whom she portrays as the most staid and lifeless of the group. The discontent that Nora projects onto the other characters is her own. Advising Marion to take action, her friend observes, " 'Shut up, Nora, I don't want anything to happen. I am perfectly all right as I am. You're talking about your-self'" (14). The displacement of her own desires is hinted at as well in her references to writing, which she views as evidence of the life force at work. Her ambivalence toward the life force, though, is evident in her praising it in others, although she tries to suppress it in herself by writ-ing the novel. She admits that she has only given the measurements of Leslie's penis because "I need to stand up to the Life Force and confine it in inches, give it a practical, conceivable measurement. Leslie Beck's laughable Life Force. If I laugh it's only to get through my days with Ed" (89). Nora purports to have a satisfying relationship with her hus-band, Ed, but clearly she is dissatisfied in the marriage. Even more, she lacks self-fulfillment and has found in her experience of the life force with Leslie only a temporary stay against that inner discontent: "But a man can thrust and thrust and have the biggest organ in the world, and survey and search the soft and convoluted foldings of female flesh for ever, in and out, in and out, and still not find what he's looking for. Any more than I was satisfied; than a thousand orgasms would have satisfied me: each could stop the clock for a moment: suspend time: unite me to the universe; block out the mind, expand the spirit, exhaust the will; but strength and sanity return: I have stopped; the clock has not: two hours nearer death and mortality is as real as ever" (107).

The novel begins with the return of Leslie into the circle. After his second wife, Anita, dies, he brings one of her paintings to Marion's art gallery, requesting that she enter it in a show. Nora tells of this incident from Marion's point of view, though she has received "the account of it only from Rosalie, mind you, to whom Marion related it over the phone, in some agitation: and the event has had to be filtered through first Marion's then Rosalie's head, and the further distortion and exaggera-tion that I suppose must happen as I, Nora, commit it to paper. Though I don't want to admit that" (9). Nora's initial introduction of herself as author along with her admission that she is reliant on hearsay for much of her account establishes the self-conscious style of the novel. Her reconstruction of the group's past is both a confessional and an interpre-tation: the accuracy of events is overshadowed by the emotions and lim-ited perception of the storyteller. Reality is less structured by memory than psychological effects, and truth is to be found in the creative work where myth resides. Leslie is the mythical figure who inspires Nora, an exemplar of the life-giving force that propels her writing. Julie Nash points out that Leslie's "appeal is not based on innate animal sexuality, or even his 'magnificent dong,' but rather the imaginations of women like Nora who need to create a trickster figure in Leslie to animate their own unsatisfactory lives" (Barreca, 100).

Weldon's description of the intertwining lives of the characters goes beyond earlier attempts to show the interrelationships of couples. The characters, although fallible, are likable. Though they err, they lack malevolence, even Leslie Beck, who, though lacking conscience, motivates the others to embrace passion in their lives. All the couples have committed infidelities with other members of the group, yet they attempt to live decent lives, raising their children with kindness and the knowledge they have at the time. Educated and urbane, they "went to the theatre, read novels, talked politics, waxed indignant, followed the news, listened to the radio; were active men and women in the PTA; brought our children up to be non-racist, non-sexist . . . and to empathise with others" (118). *Life Force* demonstrates generosity toward the characters, especially the men, lacking the parodic, satiric tone of earlier novels, contemplating the issue of right action in a complex world. For this reason, the novel is less didactic about the conditions of male privilege over female and ponders the quandary of balancing self-content with loyalty to others. Betrayal of friends and spouses predominates and is disavowed, but desire is also given credence as impulsive actions arise from the need to experience life's fullness. Suppressing desire is not a corrective and may lead to discontent and boredom as evidenced by Nora who longs for action.

Leslie's reentrance into Nora's life revives her memories of their summer together, and she longs for the intensity of feeling that she found in their sexual play. The book becomes a form of sexual expression as she attempts to find some satisfaction through the act of writing. Sex and art, arising from the same life force, then, are closely aligned. The painting that inspires Nora's story, for example, is of Leslie and Anita's bedroom, a place where Nora and others have made love to him. Adopting Marion's persona, she sublimates her desire for Leslie. Viewing Marion as cold and capable of resisting Leslie's vigorous magnetism, Nora depicts her friend as sexually uninterested and ambitious. Nora uses Marion's persona as a defense against her feelings, another way she has of controlling the life force. Thus art becomes a sublimation of desire, which, nonetheless, finds voice in the paradoxical effort to suppress it. Nora also feels guilty about the affair, especially that she has kept it secret from her husband, Ed. By adopting Marion's point of view, or

Marion's voice, she can distance the guilt as well. She says, for example, that she doesn't think Marion experiences guilt (27).

Nora tries to capture the point of view of Marion because she sees her as unaffected by Leslie's seductive personality. She interprets Marion's sexual relationship with Leslie as born of economic necessity, as she speaks through Marion's voice: "There was some quality in Leslie's sexual energy, his very indomitability, the size and scope of the tool fate had given him, that failed to ignite the erotic imagination: or at any rate mine. I could take or leave this experience, and it paid the rent" (138–39). In addition, Marion hasn't given up her life for husband and children: she is a single, childless woman who is also a successful art dealer. On the other hand, Nora's life has been dedicated to husband and children. While her analysis of Marion may seem critical, she in fact admires her friend's ability to place herself outside the world of men, which subsumes Nora. In contrast to Nora's infatuation with Leslie, Marion arranges a business deal to have his baby and then sell the infant to a South African couple. With a half million dollars from the sale of her child, Marion buys a gallery and is launched into a successful career as an art dealer. It is this story that Nora finds fascinating because it reflects the obverse of her own dull, passionless life.

By writing her story, Nora changes her life, as actions do have consequences. No longer able to resist seeing Leslie, she takes action and visits him, lying to Ed regarding her whereabouts. Leslie takes her upstairs to Anita's attic studio, where she finds that the dead woman's paintings are all about Leslie, depicting the diverse places he had made love to the women of the circle. He tells Nora, " 'I was her muse. . . . It was her Life Force, not mine' " (171). Nora finds gratification when Leslie selects as his favorite painting that of a platform on the fourth story of an unfinished building, a place where the two of them had made love. She feels "a sense of pre-eminence, of being something special" (171). Leslie's compliment gives Nora a new feeling of self-worth. Suddenly, she feels valued by the life force.

Her visit to Leslie's studio, though life-affirming, has the effect of destroying Nora's marriage: when Ed discovers her deception, he leaves her. By taking action (visiting Leslie), Nora evokes the life force, which releases her from her unhappy marriage. Returning to Leslie's house, she enters using her old key and sets fire to the studio. By burning the paintings, she figuratively ends Leslie Beck's hold over her and the others, bringing an end to the novel. But Nora has not finished her novel, and in a final flourish she creates a happy ending for all; in the final pages, however, she admits that although this satisfying ending is fictional, "Leslie Beck is true. Leslie Beck the Magnificent; Leslie Beck and his Life Force, moving through our lives, leaping, unstoppable, like electricity, from this one to that one, burning us up, wearing us out, making us old, passing on, its only purposes its own survival. Leslie Beck, enemy of death, bringer of life: the best thing that ever happened to us" (200). Life is not art and human beings do not act like characters in a book. But the artist remains to capture the resounding life force that motivates human desire and action that give meaning to life.

Growing Rich

Growing Rich centers on the lives of three 16-year-old girls—Carmen, Annie, and Laura—who have grown up in the small town of Fenedge. Their desire to get out of the town creates the complications of the plot as they try to overcome impediments to their leaving. The girls' dreams are dashed when they fail their exams, which they had hoped would facilitate their escape. Hattie, the narrator, suffers from neurological damage to her spine; unable to walk she spends her days looking out her window in Landsfield Crescent, a housing project where the girls also live. Because of her physical disability, Hattie becomes an avid voyeur, observing the young women attempting to escape their desolate lives. As the girls' confidante, she relates their story, drawing attention to the layered perceptions that her account holds. Hattie is one of Weldon's most skillfully drawn narrators, capable of imagining what the other characters are thinking or doing. Though she claims that "[t]his is not my story," she is an engaging character in her own right. When she strays off into accounts of her life we wonder how she has suffered the neurological damage. Tied to her wheelchair and window, Hattie enjoys little mobility except for her trips to the Otherly Abled Center, where she continues to observe the town's activities. Like Maia in *The President's Child,* she gives voice to the trials of the female characters.

This environment of desperation invites the presence of the Devil, who appears as a driver for a wealthy man, Bernard Bellamy. The Devil greatly resembles Joyce Carol Oates's Arnold Friend in "Where Are You Going, Where Have You Been?" Driving a BMW, "he was an old-young man with startlingly blue eyes; he wore a navy blue military-style uniform and a chauffeur's cap which cast a shadow over a strong, bony

face" (2–3). Like Arnold Friend, the driver wears a costume that facilitates his deception as he drives around, trying to buy the souls of others,
especially that of Carmen. Carmen's susceptibility to the Devil's over-
tures derives from her virginity, her discontent, and her desire to leave
the mediocre small town of Fenedge. The novel describes the struggle
between her and the Devil as he tries to buy her soul, tempting her with
grandeur and the elimination of life's ineluctable problems. The Devil's
bargain proposes that she sleep with his employer, Sir Bernard Bellamy,
a wealthy man who is renovating Bellamy House, the "Devil's safe
house" located outside of town. The Devil's persuasion is keener because
Carmen's failure to surrender not only brings difficulties to her but to
her friends as well. To further seduce her, he occasionally bestows good
fortune to her and her friends in order to show her how problem-free life
can be. Her body, for example, undergoes changes, fulfilling an ideal
image, which makes her attractive and desirable to others. Applying for
jobs in an employment office, she suddenly experiences a physical transformation: her breasts grow from an A-cup size to a C, her waist gets
smaller and her hips larger, and her legs grow longer: "When Carmen's
name was called, and she had to stand up . . . a kind of sigh travelled
around the room. Both men and women stared. Although there was a
head-on robustness about her figure, clothed as it was in a far too tight
T-shirt and a skirt on the short side even when she'd put it on and now
shorter than ever, there was a fine-boned tranquillity about her face, as
if she'd never had to give it a second thought from the day she first
observed its perfection" (47). Later, encountering a young man she is
enamored by, Carmen discovers an ugly zit on the end of her nose,
placed there by the Devil. The Devil continues to hinder her success and
her love life while she persists in resisting his invitation.

As the driver, the Devil symbolizes the social evils that propel (drive)
stereotypes and expectations of women. The conventionally beautiful
woman has copious opportunities; the homely or unattractive one must
settle for gross labor. Carmen, for example, in her beneficent body is
offered a job as a stewardess, but her friends must settle for menial labor
in a chicken factory or at Bellamy House. When Carmen refuses the job,
her body returns to its previous unexceptional form. The Devil, then, is
women's lack of economic opportunity, the disregard for their actual
worth and the physical requirements that determine how they are valued in society. And the Devil is also associated with luck, as he tells Carmen: " 'Life's all luck, no justice. Luck has everything to do with it, so I

have everything to do with it—because the Prince of Darkness is the Prince of Luck. Too bad!' " (148). Women as a gender are out of luck in a power system that devalues them, yet some, those born beautiful or rich, have more luck than others. To make a deal with the Devil, then, is much more tempting to those born without power. Paradoxically, though, men have their power because their souls already belong to the Devil. Sir Bellamy's success has evil origins because it derives from his disregard for the environment and lack of respect for others. He renovates Bellamy House, on a shoreline, destroying the environment and ecological homes of endangered species. Much is made in the novel of the economic benefits of jobs and the countervailing harm done to the environment. Bellamy's destruction, for profit, of the environment reflects the evils of a shortsighted society that values money over nature. This point is further made when a worker discovers on the property the graves of women who have been killed as witches. Bellamy turns this disadvantageous situation into a profit by selling the remains to archaeologists, who remove them, desecrating the sacred burial ground. Thus, the Devil operates by offering financial rewards that preclude our compassion for the powerless—nature and women.

As Carmen's friends' lives disintegrate, they compel her to give in to the Driver, but she continues to refuse. It is only when Annie is dying of anorexia that Carmen succumbs and agrees to sleep with Sir Bellamy. Carmen sacrifices her own soul for the life of a friend, an act of goodness that brings about her salvation. True to Weldon's plot turns that favor her heroines, Sir Bellamy cannot perform sexually and instead asks Carmen to marry him. Carmen's beneficence pays off and she receives all that she had hoped for—money and love. Sir Bellamy, too, benefits because as he has told the Devil earlier, " 'It was her soul I responded to' " (193). The soul that Bellamy refers to is that of Carmen's real self, not her physical, virginal body. Both Sir Bellamy and Carmen escape the grasp of the Devil because of good actions. Even if the Devil has preeminence in real life, he can be defeated within the confines of the novel.

The town, too, receives the bounty of the couple's union, the lives of its inhabitants improving for the better, including Hattie's; she is miraculously cured by a doctor's assistant who pops her back after she has fallen: "Now I don't know what happened. Perhaps the paralysis was indeed hysterical; perhaps the Chicago neural graft had finally done its work; perhaps some disc in my backbone, which had been causing the trouble, was released: perhaps the benefit which flowed from Carmen's assent to her own female nature flowed into me as well—though what feminist would want to hear that?" (237). Hattie is healed of her ailment, her spinelessness, when Carmen eludes the Devil and is rewarded with love and money. Hattie's paralysis represents that of all women who have been disabled by their culture because of their gender. Hattie, for example, suffered neurological damage to her spine when "complications following a botched pregnancy termination required emergency invasive surgery, and a wasp bit the knife-wielding hand mid-stroke and a section of my neural fibre was inadvertently severed" (205). The serio-comic symbolism here is clear: gender is a fateful sting that leaves women socially paralyzed. Women's biology, signified in Hattie's abortion, has weakened them; and they must, if you will, stand up for themselves. The spine, signifying strength, regenerates as women overcome their social disabilities through determination and the support of one another.

In *Growing Rich* Weldon returns to familiar patterns incorporating the interlaced lives of female friends and their idiosyncratic, sometimes neglectful parents. The tone here though is lighter and more playful, and the allegorical structure sets realism on its ear. One significant difference in the girls' relationship is that they are supportive of one another, lacking the acrimony we have seen in other female relationships. Further, the families, although dysfunctional, are amusing rather than repugnant. In contrast to Carmen, her parents are slobs, slovenly and obese, who live in filth and disarray: "The cat's food hardened, maggoty, in a saucer uncleaned for days; dirty dishes piled in the sink; the smell of frying fish lingered in the air; little dusty yellow globules of fat spotted the ceiling above the cooker" (15).

Growing Rich is a tale about the evils of a society enraptured by image and money. The Devil surely resides in the desire for power that supplants human compassion. Similarly, the world of nature is also left out of the financial equation. Birds, plants, and animals have no voice in this world, even less of a voice than women, who at least triumph in this fairy tale. The Devil is effectively banished when Sir Bellamy insists that Carmen speak for the environment, but the Devil's safe house remains, as Hattie concludes, "I would like to report that the Devil's safe house burnt down: was razed to the ground. . . . But it would not be true. Bellamy House still stands, and makes a decent profit, and nothing exciting or remarkable seems to happen there. But then nothing exciting ever happens in Fenedge these days. A tradition has grown up that you must never insult the town aloud, or hope too vehemently to escape it, in case the Devil happens to be flying by, and overhears, and all hell breaks loose" (250). Weldon leaves us with a perfect world that at any time could be disturbed by the presence of the Devil, who thrives on discontent and complacency. Carmen's resistance, though, is a guide: be courageous and give in to evil forces only out of compassion and perhaps the Devil will be thwarted. By telling her story, Hattie brings an end to her paralysis. Carmen's actions strengthen the entire cast of women, offering a happy ending to those who stand up against a social establishment that oppresses women.

Chapter Eight
The Trouble with Marriage

Marriage is a terrible intertwining, a fearful osmosis; I will have to relearn myself. (*Worst Fears*, 66)

Weldon's last three novels portray women in bad marriages with husbands who betray, deride, and abandon them. In *Splitting* the protagonist, Angelica Rice, is turned out of her home because her husband believes her to have had a relationship with one of the couple's friends. Ostracized and penniless, she literally splits apart, manifesting personalities that, working together, enable her to survive her husband's abandonment and attempt to defame her. In *Trouble* (published as *Affliction* in England), the husband of pregnant Annette quite suddenly after 10 years of marriage begins to treat her cruelly, taking the advice of his kooky astrological psychotherapist, who convinces him that she is mad. *Worst Fears* relates the shocking discoveries of a woman whose husband has died of a heart attack. She encounters the lovers of her philandering husband, one of whom is her best friend, and is told that she has no rights to their property, having never been legally married to him.

What these books have in common is the feckless husband whose wife suffers from his indiscretions and dishonesty. In divorce, women are at a disadvantage, faced with lawyers who are hired to tell lies about them. Women who allow their husbands to play the traditional role of money and property manager are foolishly deceived. The protagonists' relegation of financial matters to their husbands has disastrous effects. Yet they overcome, finding a way out of the financial and emotional morass that tries to destroy them—a way out through revenge or by simply taking control of their lives.

Splitting

Splitting, nominated for the Whitbread Prize, extends a metaphor dealt with more subtly in other novels, the fragmented identity of women. These fractured selves include the identities formulated by social expectations and those internalized ones that women repress fearing rejection and alienation. These divisions of personality appear in previous novels in which compliant wives become prostitutes, as in *Praxis,* or innocent girls become vindictive witches, as in *Words of Advice.* In *Splitting,* Weldon plays with the idea of multiple personalities, borrowing the psychological concept as a poetic device, creating Lady Angelica Rice, whose hidden identities reveal themselves after a painful divorce. Weldon has described her own experience of multiple selves: "[T]he writing of fiction, for me, is the splitting of the self into myriad parts. It's being author, characters, readers, everyone" (Wandor, 162).

Before meeting her husband, Edwin, Lady Rice was Angelica, a rock singer. After her marriage she took on the role of a proper English wife living on an estate outside the village of Barley. This persona has had the effect of hiding not only the former Angelica, but all the counterparts that make up her identity. At the estate she lives a superficial life, socializing with a coterie of people who sexually intermingle, reminiscent of *Life Force,* leaving and returning to their marriages, bickering and harboring resentments for other members of the group. Lady Rice is fairly innocent of these events, and as a result becomes a victim of the group's deceptive, philandering entanglements. Taking one of the men in one night after his wife has run off with another man, she falls asleep beside him on the bed. Discovering them there, Edwin accuses her of infidelity and throws her out. Outcast, she moves into a hotel and gets a job as the secretary of Edwin's lawyer, Brian Moss. Angelica tries to ignore the voices of her multiple selves when they emerge: "She has tried to incorporate these bickering women, these alter egos, back into herself; now she tries to regain her sense of self, but she can't. She must listen to them, and answer them" (123).

Central to the emerging personalities is Jelly White, the efficient, organized secretary who begins to interfere with the correspondence between her lawyer and Brian Moss. Jelly goes beyond the stereotypical, self-serving secretary; she is the survivor of the group, who tends to Angelica's financial interests while the others express different aspects of her personality. Besides Lady Rice and Jelly, there is Angel, the sex-crazed one who unabashedly seduces the chauffeur, Ram, and Ajax, a male counterpart. Through subterfuge Angelica, with the help of Jelly, reclaims her rights as a divorcée, acquiring a generous settlement and running off with the chauffeur. She is a new woman, pieced back together, fully intact. It is through splitting apart that Angelica is able to find coherence. She succeeds in unifying these disparate identities when she strikes out against the male world by resisting her ex-husband's attempts to deprive her of money and by discovering and embracing the hidden selves within. Incorporating her personalities she runs off with Ram to create a new life for herself.

Trouble

Trouble stands out from Weldon's previous novels in its almost complete lack of authorial narration, its story developed primarily through dialogue between the characters. The reading experience is akin to watching a drama develop, with episodic events that draw us into the novel's tragicomedy. Annette, the pregnant wife, is troubled by her husband, Spicer, who after 10 years of marriage has become intensely critical of her behavior and sexually abusive. Convinced by Spicer that she is going insane, Annette tolerates his behavior. Gradually she realizes that he is under the influence of a pop psychologist who specializes in astrological psychotherapy. At the novel's close she discovers that Dr. Rhea Marks has, through hypnosis, turned him against her. The novel is a powerful tragicomedy in its outlandish portrayal of Dr. Rhea—and her Jungian therapy— who along with her psychiatrist husband, preys on unwary patients. The tragedy is contained not only in Annette's acceptance of her husband's abuse but also in her baby's death.

Spicer uses the astrological term "afflicted" to describe Annette's flawed personality: "You are badly afflicted in both the Fourth and Seventh houses. The house of childhood and the house of marriage. The unhappy, lonely child of elderly parents, a mother badly treated by a faithless husband—we know all that to be true, don't we? . . . you're so confused, hardly anything registers. Look at us. Your total lack of sensitivity" (51). Clearly Spicer is the afflicted one, having been brainwashed by the Markses, sodomizing Annette, taking pleasure in her pain, and telling her to turn over and talk into the pillow while they are having sex. These episodes of sadomasochism, written as dialogue, capture the dark side of marriage, as Spicer fundamentally rapes his wife and she makes excuses for him to her friend Gilda. In a conversation between the friends, Gilda remarks: 'You mean upsetting and hurting you is what turns him on?' 'It isn't like that, Gilda. I think it was because I wouldn't let him do what he wanted that he went to see Dr. Rhea Marks in the first place' " (114).

In this novel's depiction of marriage, Weldon takes the reader behind closed doors, portraying human behavior at its worst. *Trouble*'s realistic details and dialogue succeed in creating a troubling portrait of a marriage. After losing the baby, Annette has a bout of madness, absently wandering away, hitchhiking with strangers. Raped by one, she falls into a ditch and is rescued by a rural couple. Describing the experience to Gilda, she metaphorically describes the ditch as a gap: "The true gap is the space between the world as it ought to be and the world as it is; between what you think love and marriage and babies are going to be and what it turns out to be and its proper name is Disappointment. Anyone can fall into it, Gilda. It's horrible down here" (218). In these poignant lines, Annette sums up the experience of a host of Weldon heroines, but like others, she finds her way out of the gap. Giving up on Spicer, she finds a new love who will help her "keep what belongs to the past in the past" (227).

By adopting Spicer's views, Anita succumbs to a male definition of her reality. Refusing to look closely at the events around her, she makes excuses for her husband, lacking faith in her own capacity to understand the world. She ignores Gilda's sage advice and remains oblivious to her own needs and those of the child she is carrying. Weldon suggests in this novel that women must learn to trust their own perceptions and to resist the story of their oppressors. Lacking self-esteem, Anita readily accepts her husband's abuse and his absurd version of reality. Because she remains blind to her own needs and those of the child, she loses the baby and falls into the pit of disappointment from which she must ascend in order to reconstruct her view of reality.

Worst Fears

Marital problems in *Worst Fears* arise after the death of the husband, Ned, a theater critic and philanderer. At the novel's beginning, his wife Alexandra, a well-known British actress, is unaware of her husband's infidelities. The worst fears the title refers to are those of Alexandra, who, while mourning for her dead husband, discovers that he has had extramarital relationships with acquaintances and friends in the small community of Eddon Gurney where the couple own a country home. With an omniscient narrator who focuses primarily on Alexandra's point of view, the novel absorbs the reader in a domestic mystery in which Ned's past actions are gradually revealed to us as they are to his wife. The novel is successful in creating the mystery surrounding Ned's death, complete with characters who hover about the scene with their uncertain motives. The awareness of the gossiping, intrusive community members is hidden from Alexandra, the outsider who has been living in London playing Nora in *A Doll's House,* and to the reader. Adding to the ambiguity of events is Weldon's depiction of Alexandra, whose perception is put into question by the observations of others. In her last novel to date, Weldon has successfully created multiple perspectives without the addition of objective dialogue and intrusive narration that we have seen in earlier novels. This novel has the feel of traditional realism and a quirkiness that guides the reader through psychological land mines and outright narrative trickery.

The novel begins with Alexandra's return to The Cottage at Eddon Gurney after Ned's heart attack, his body having been discovered on the dining-room floor by her friend Abbie. From the beginning Alexandra suspects something is awry with the circumstances and her friends' account of her husband's death. Prompted by her mother, Alexandra asks Abbie why she was at her home at half past five in the morning. Soon she hears a woman keening outside, a local, Jenny Linden, who declares her love for Ned. Alexandra dismisses the woman as mad, but evidence mounts that some relationship had existed between the two. Breaking into Jenny's home, Alexandra discovers pictures of her husband, his toothbrush, and a miniature replication of their bedroom. Stealing Jenny's address book and diary, she begins to try to piece together the puzzle, imagining a scenario whereby Jenny harassed Ned. Calling numbers from the address book, she still refuses to believe the truth even when Jenny's husband, Dave, tells her: "The moment you'd walk out the door she'd walk in. He died fucking her. He died fucking my wife. Too much excitement" (76).

It is only after a call to Jenny's therapist, pretending to be Jenny, that Alexandra is able to face the truth. The therapist gives her the phrase "worst fears" to deal with her distraught state, and Alexandra assumes the words are "meant to envisage the worst that could happen, and because the present didn't match up to that, feel better?" (88). In a mental exercise she describes her worst fears "that Jenny Linden is not insane, that Ned and she were having an affair, that she was in bed with him, in our brass bed into which he had invited her, and that he died fucking her, so great was his excitement and pleasure. That for a time the jerks and pantings of the dying man echoed the jerks and pantings of a joy which once I thought was reserved for me but was not; and stopped, and he was dead" (91). The exercise does have a therapeutic effect as she surrenders her illusions through voicing her fears. This admission, though, is only the beginning of Alexandra's discoveries about her marriage, as many secrets still remain. Yet Alexandra is not simply the unfortunate, betrayed wife, for she must bear some responsibility for having lived in denial, as her mother continually points out to her. Early on, the novel establishes Alexandra's inattentiveness to the world around her. Our sympathy for the bereaved wife is complicated by statements that suggest Alexandra's lack of awareness, as she remembers, for example, Ned saying to friends, "Oh, Alexandra is so unobservant for such a clever person" (94). The death of her husband forces Alexandra to come out of her self-created darkness and begin to observe the ongoing events around her. By solving the mystery of Ned's demise, she must delve into her own psychology, growing in awareness as she unveils the illusory nature of her marriage. Continuing to voice her worst fears, she gets to the core of her own self-deceptions. Fearing that Ned loved Jenny Linden, she realizes "[t]hat in the belief that a woman had to be beautiful, and sensuous, and witty, and wonderful, in order to trigger real love, erotic love, the kind of emotional drama that ran through to the heart of the universe, the hot line to the source of life itself, the in-love kind, Alexandra had been wrong. More she had shown herself to be vain, and foolish and shallow, and Ned had noticed" (166). Through self-analysis Alexandra begins to undo the misconceptions on which she has based her personality. If Ned has loved the unattractive, hysterical Jenny Linden, then Alexandra's beauty, sophistication, and fame lack the significance she has given them.

Through skillful plotting, revelations begin to surface and Alexandra's first summation of her worst fears turns out to be meager ruminations in comparison to her husband's actual betrayals. Compounding these discoveries is her realization that not only is she being deceived by the locals and friends, but she is the subject of their derision and resentment. Ned and others have believed she has had an affair with her costar and that he has fathered her child, Sascha. (In truth she had one failed sexual bout with the man and in fact he is gay.) Her brother-in-law Hamish, for example, turns on her at one point, and she realizes that he doesn't like her. Diamond the dog growls at her, privy to secrets that she has yet to realize. That Alexandra has less awareness than the household dog is a comical jab at her gross self-absorption, and her desire to avoid self-analysis is expressed when she kicks at Diamond and considers giving him away. Similarly, she tries to rid herself of Jenny by kicking her and throwing her out of the house. Alexandra suffers from her misplaced aggressions as she discovers that Ned's infidelity was not singular, but included trysts with the actress who has taken her place in *A Doll's House* and even her best friend, Abbie, who was in bed with Ned when he died. Sexual indiscretions are matched by financial ones: Ned has willed Jenny Linden The Cottage, and the London apartment returns to the ownership of his former wife. Further, Ned had never received a divorce from his first wife, rendering Alexandra's marriage a farce.

The excessive betrayals and revelations that Alexandra experiences finally have the effect of dismantling her old self and perceptions. Discovering that Jenny has ownership of The Cottage is the coup de grâce that allows her to begin a new life. She finds in the expression "best wishes" a way to say good-bye to Ned and to let go of her anger: "Alexandra offered her best wishes to Ned. She could see he was badly in need of them. She could not offer him forgiveness, since there was no such thing. Best wishes she could manage. If Ned had believed Sascha was not his son, if Ned believed the betrayal was hers, Alexandra's, then he was not so much to blame: she must have appeared as hateful to him as he had lately to her. More fool he that he had let Jenny Linden persuade him of it, more tragic for him, and her, Alexandra, that he had died believing. A sore point in the universe which could never heal: a wound forever open" (187).

Like Nora in *Life Force* Alexandra destroys the myth that has led her through the labyrinth of falsehoods revealed by her husband's death. Before Jenny can take possession of The Cottage, Alexandra sets it on fire, which turns out to be unnecessary as it is struck by lightning soon after. Margaret Mitchell comments on Weldon heroines who burn down their houses: "It is a symbolic gesture with considerable literary resonance, for the house is the most tangible symbol of the myth of bourgeois domesticity. To burn it down can be seen as the ultimate act of protest against the perpetuation of that myth" (Mitchell, 539). Leaving the myth behind she begins a new life allowing that "she could, but would not, best-wish Jenny Linden. She must be allowed some indulgence, some caprice. And she best-wished Ned again, because what was the point of not? Ned was dead. And she was off" (200). Thus Alexandra is rewarded by the author for having gone through the maze of difficulties and recognizing her own failures of observation, best-wishing almost everyone including her friend Abbie, affirming once again the importance of female friendship.

The wives of these novels lose their former sense of identity to achieve self-understanding and autonomy. Alexandra in *Worst Fears* and Anita in *Trouble* wrestle with the construction of their worldview and find a new sense of self. Angelica in *Splitting* must in effect fall apart before she finds autonomy. We see in these last three novels a shift of emphasis in Weldon's vision, from the inequities of economic and ideological constraints that women suffer to the importance of self-examination that women must undergo to wrest themselves from destructive relationships. This latter theme has always been present in Weldon's fiction, but in these examples she describes the difficult journey to self-discovery that women must embrace to take control of their lives. Freedom comes through self-awareness and self-confidence, Weldon implies. This message is one of empowerment and shows a growth in the author's vision of female experience.

Conclusion

Fay Weldon chronicles the lives of women, unveiling the cultural mythos that both defines their social identity and inhibits their ability to find personal autonomy. Weldon treats these matters with wry humor and goodwill. The author's loyalty to describing the plight of women in a culture of male privilege explains her vision at least on one level. Not only does she give us keen portrayals of female experience, she also offers a great deal to narrative inventions that transcend subject matter. Weldon's experimentation with the novel's form is ambitious and satisfying. She surprises her readers with language that defies propriety. She unsettles the "truth" of perception by giving attention to multiple points of view. But even more, she makes us look at human relationships and the interactions that encompass our everyday lives.

Weldon's fiction purveys the world of domesticity and work, describing the interchanges that occur in the living room, bedroom, and workplace. Forswearing a romanticized view of life's realities, she brings the ludicrous and the urbane to our attention, showing us where we spend most of our time. Her vision is incisive and revelatory, a viewpoint that sees the dark and light within the common scene. Finally, her honesty about human behavior and motives gives energy to her plot constructions and viability to her themes and concerns.

Weldon is enigmatic to those who seek to understand her. Though her loyalty to female experience is consistent, she offers no clear answers to ethical questions, with the exception of the abuse of power. When reading Weldon, one does not sense that she is trying to conform to a literary tradition. She writes about what is important to her, turning a cold shoulder to literary categories. Reading her works is a plunging into the real, an account of how people speak and act in a modern world. Describing our relationships with one another and our treatment of children, she offers unflattering portraits of ourselves. Yet she also expresses faith in the human potential for change. She places our lives within a luminous frame and asks us to look closely. Fay Weldon writes stories that remind us of our human kinship, painting us as both flawed and redeemable, capturing the essential quality of our existence, as if indeed she knew us.

Notes and References

Preface

1. Richard Todd, "The Presence of Postmodernism in British Fiction: Aspects of Style and Selfhood," in *Approaching Postmodernism: Papers Presented on Postmodernism,* ed. Douwe Fokkema and Hans Bertens (Utrecht: Utrecht Publishers, 1986), 104–5.

2. Agate Krouse, "Feminism and Art in Fay Weldon's Novels," *Critique,* no. 2 (1978): 20; hereafter cited in text.

3. John Haffenden, *Novelists in Interview* (New York: Methuen, 1985), 313; hereafter cited in text.

Chapter One

1. Regina Barreca, *Fay Weldon's Wicked Fictions* (Hanover, N.H.: University Press of New England, 1994), 6; hereafter cited in text.

2. Elisabeth Dunn, "Among the Women . . ." *Telegraph Sunday Magazine,* December 16, 1979, 58; hereafter cited in text.

3. John Heilpern, "Facts of Female Life," *Observer,* February 18, 1979, 33.

4. Margaret Mitchell, "Fay Weldon," in *British Writers,* ed. George Stade and Carol Howard (New York: Simon & Schuster, 1997), 521; hereafter cited in text.

5. All quotes from Weldon's works are cited in text by page number. Please refer to the bibliography for information on Weldon's books published in the United States; these are the editions cited throughout this text.

6. David Lodge, *The Art of Fiction* (New York: Viking, 1992), 127; hereafter cited in text.

7. John Braine, "A Natural Novelist," *Books and Bookmen* (January 1977): 28.

8. Michelene Wandor, *On Gender and Writing* (London: Pandora Press, 1983), 163; hereafter cited in text.

9. Ann Marie Hebert, "Rewriting the Feminine Script: Fay Weldon's Wicked Laughter," *Critical Matrix* 7, no. 1 (1993): 28; hereafter cited in text.

10. Mina Kumar, "Interview," *Belles Lettres: A Review of Books by Women* 10, no. 2 (1995): 16; hereafter cited in text.

Chapter Two

    1.   Patricia Waugh, *Feminist Fiction: Revisiting the Postmodern* (New York: Routledge, 1989), 195.

Chapter Four

    1.   Olga Kenyon, *Women Novelists Today* (New York: St. Martin's Press, 1988), 119; hereafter cited in text.

Chapter Five

    1.   Cliff Terry, "Interview," *Chicago Tribune,* March 18, 1990, 4.
    2.   Iris Murdoch, "Against Dryness," *Encounter* 16 (1961): 20.

Selected Bibliography

PRIMARY SOURCES

. . . *And the Wife Ran Away*. New York: McKay, 1967.
Down Among the Women. New York: St. Martin's, 1972.
Female Friends. Chicago: Academy Chicago Publishers, 1974.
Remember Me. New York: Random House, 1976.
Words of Advice. New York: Random House, 1977.
Praxis. New York: Summit, 1978.
Puffball. New York: Summit, 1980.
Watching Me, Watching You. 1981.
The President's Child. New York: Doubleday, 1983.
The Life and Loves of a She-Devil: New York: Random House, 1983.
Letters to Alice: On First Reading Jane Austen. New York: Taplinger, 1985.
Polaris. London: Hodder & Stoughton, 1985.
The Shrapnel Academy. New York: Viking, 1986.
The Heart of the Country. New York: Viking, 1987.
The Hearts and Lives of Men. New York: Viking, 1987.
The Leader of the Band. New York: Viking, 1988.
The Cloning of Joanna May. London: Collins, 1989.
Darcy's Utopia. New York: Viking, 1990.
Growing Rich. London: HarperCollins, 1992.
Life Force. New York: HarperCollins, 1992.
Trouble. New York: Viking, 1993.
Splitting. New York: Atlantic Monthly Press, 1995.
Worst Fears. New York: Atlantic Monthly Press, 1996.
Wicked Women. New York: Atlantic Monthly Press, 1997.

SECONDARY SOURCES

Barreca, Regina. *Fay Weldon's Wicked Fictions*. Hanover, N.H.: University Press of New England, 1994.
Braine, John. "A Natural Novelist." *Books and Bookmen* (January 1977): 28.
Dunn, Elizabeth. "Among the Women. . . ." *Telegraph Sunday Magazine,* December 16, 1979, 55 – 64.
Haffenden, John. *Novelists in Interview*. New York: Methuen, 1985.

Hebert, Ann Marie. "Rewriting the Feminine Script: Fay Weldon's Wicked Laughter." *Critical Matrix* 7, no. 1 (1993): 21–40.

Heilpern, John. "Facts of Female Life." *Observer* (February 18, 1979): 33.

Kenyon, Olga. *Women Novelists Today.* New York: St. Martin's Press, 1988.

Krouse, Agate Nesaule. "Feminism and Art in Fay Weldon's Novel." *Critique* 20, no. 2 (1978): 5–20.

Kumar, Mina. "Interview." *Belles Lettres: A Review of Books by Women* 10, no. 2 (1995): 16–18.

Lodge, David. *The Art of Fiction.* New York: Viking, 1992.

Mitchell, Margaret E. "Fay Weldon." In *British Writers,* ed. George Stade and Carol Howard. New York: Simon & Schuster, 1997.

Murdoch, Iris. "Against Dryness." *Encounter* 16 (1961): 16–20.

Terry, Cliff. "Interview." *Chicago Tribune* (March 18, 1990): 4.

Todd, Richard. "The Presence of Postmodernism in British Fiction: Aspects of Style and Selfhood." In *Approaching Postmodernism: Papers Presented on Postmodernism,* ed. Douwe Fokkema and Hans Bertens. Utrecht: Utrecht Publishers, 1986.

Wandor, Michelene. *On Gender and Writing.* London: Pandora Press, 1983.

Waugh, Patricia. *Feminine Fiction: Revisiting the Postmodern.* New York: Routledge, 1989.

Index

The Author

Lana Faulks is a visiting lecturer at the University of Oklahoma. She received her doctorate from the University of Florida, where she specialized in the modern British novel.

The Editor

Kinley E. Roby is professor emeritus of English at Northeastern University. He is the twentieth-century field editor of Twayne's English Authors Series, series editor of Twayne's Critical History of British Drama, and general editor of Twayne's Women and Literature Series. He has written books on Arnold Bennett, Edward VII, and Joyce Cary, and edited a collection of essays on T. S. Eliot. He makes his home in Naples, Florida.